always up to date

The law changes, but Nolo is on top of it! We offer several ways to make sure you and your Nolo products are up to date:

1 **Nolo's Legal Updater**
We'll send you an email whenever a new edition of this book is published! Sign up at **www.nolo.com/legalupdater**.

2 **Updates @ Nolo.com**
Check **www.nolo.com/update** to find recent changes in the law that affect the current edition of your book.

3 **Nolo Customer Service**
To make sure that this edition of the book is the most recent one, call us at **800-728-3555** and ask one of our friendly customer service representatives. Or find out at **www.nolo.com**.

please note

We believe accurate, plain-English legal information should help you solve many of your own legal problems. But this text is not a substitute for personalized advice from a knowledgeable lawyer. If you want the help of a trained professional—and we'll always point out situations in which we think that's a good idea—consult an attorney licensed to practice in your state.

Always Dad

Being a Great Father
During & After Divorce

DATE DUE			
	By Paul Mandelstein		

261-9500 PRINTED IN U.S.A.

NOLO

FIRST EDITION	May 2006
EDITOR	Emily Doskow
PRODUCTION	Susan Putney
DESIGN	Susan Putney
COVER	Susan Putney
PROOFREADER	Sara Tolchin
INDEX	Medea Minnich
PRINTING	Consolidated Printers, Inc.

Mandelstein, Paul.
  Always dad : being a great dad during & after divorce / by Paul Mandelstein.-- 1st ed.
    p. cm.
  ISBN 1-4133-0495-8 (alk. paper)
    1. Divorced fathers--United States--Psychology. 2. Divorce--United States. 3. Father
and child--United States. I. Title: Being a great dad during & after divorce. II. Title.
HQ756.M3424 2006
306.8920851--dc22

2006040103

Because of great love,
one is courageous.

—LAO TZU

Dedicated to the memory of my friend Laura E. Hammond Farrow, an expert mediator whose compassion and ethics in work and relationships were an example of a life nobly lived.

Acknowledgments

Many fathers, mothers, children, therapists and doctors, lawyers and clergy have contributed their stories of struggle, transformation, and hard-won understanding to this book. Although they remain unnamed, to all of them I am truly thankful.

My sincere appreciations to Hal Zina Bennett, my writing partner, for making this book come alive with wit, wisdom, and clarity. And many thanks to Charles Drucker, my good friend and colleague, for contributing his unwavering editorial guidance and forward-thinking advice to this project.

Thanks to Emily Doskow and Mary Randolph, my editors at Nolo, who devoted their editorial skills and legal expertise to making *Always Dad* a lively, comprehensive, factual, and easy-to-follow book.

To my children, Zachary, Naomi, and Nicolas, for struggling through the divorce process and remaining upbeat and family-positive in spite of it. To their mother and my former wife, Cornelia, thank you for these wonderful children. For that I am eternally grateful to you.

To Judy, my better half and the love of my life, my words fall short describing how your encouragement, support, and belief in me made this meaningful project come to fruition. And to Judy's son, Jason, thanks for being reasonably easygoing about me, the new man in your mother's life and in yours.

Table of Contents

CHAPTER THREE
Daily Life as a Single Dad

CHAPTER FOUR
The Noncustodial Dance

CHAPTER FIVE
Ex-Communications:
10 Ways to Make Talking to Your Ex Easier

CHAPTER SIX

Settling Up: Legal and Custody Issues

CHAPTER SEVEN

Let's Get Real About the Kids

CHAPTER EIGHT

Keeping Yourself Together

CHAPTER NINE

Birthdays and Holidays

CHAPTER TEN

Kids, Friends, Dating, and Lovers

CHAPTER ELEVEN

Taking a Chance on Love Again:
Remarriage and Blending Families

APPENDIX

Divorce and Fathering Resources

INDEX

Lemons into Lemonade

Breaking Up Is Hard to Do

On our wedding day, most of us believe that the marriage will last forever. Unfortunately, many marriages end in divorce—fewer than 25% of all family units in the United States today are traditional nuclear families. If your marriage is headed for a divorce, you have my sympathy. I've been through it myself and know the challenges you are facing. This is a time of high anxiety, when fear, frustration, disappointment, resentment, and anger hover at the edges of our consciousness, sometimes prompting us to say or do things we later regret. Let's face it: even if you're the one seeking the divorce, you will not avoid feelings of loss, hurt, and confusion. This is particularly true when you are a parent and your children are suffering as a result of the decisions you and your spouse have made.

When one door closes, another door opens; but we so often look so long and so regretfully upon the closed door, that we do not see the ones which open for us."

—ALEXANDER GRAHAM BELL

When the mother of my three children and I divorced after nearly 17 years of marriage, my first few evenings away from the marriage bed were full of conflicted feelings: relief, confusion, sadness, and panic. I was relieved that I was no longer sleeping next to someone with whom I had irreconcilable differences. At the same time I was deeply distressed about not being with my children, who were 15, 13, and 8, on a daily basis. Missing my daughter's first dress-up date made me quite sad, and learning about my youngest son's uncomfortable encounter with a panhandler had me concerned about his day-to-day safety. And my relationship with my soon-to-be-ex-wife had become one of continual conflict, misunderstood communications, and abruptly ending phone calls. I needed help accepting my new realities, and turning these sour lemons into sweet lemonade seemed like a distant dream.

A Chance for Growth

I began speaking with many fathers, mothers, children, and extended family members who had been affected by divorce. I soon realized that my own cautionary tales and the unvarnished details of other families' divorces could be helpful in guiding other fathers through similar challenges.

It also occurred to me that perhaps we could approach the process in a more positive way than previous generations did. Why couldn't we view divorce as a path for personal healing and growth for ourselves and everyone else involved? Might it pave the way for a much more positive and healthy transition? Clearly, divorce is an unfortunate and troubling event, not anyone's first choice of a life change. But like other challenges, we would do well to find a way through it that could help us develop practices for making our lives better.

I came to believe that the concept of the divorced family as "broken" is obsolete. In truth, a family that stays in a bad marriage is a broken family, and divorce can be the way to move beyond that unhappy state. It's time to reframe our attitudes toward divorce and look at ways to nurture the "extended" family—a more accurate and positive term to describe a post-divorce family.

In the course of thinking about divorce and working with fathers, I founded *Father.com* and the *Father Resource Network (FRN)*, a non-profit organization, offering programs and support to help fathers with the challenges of parenting and divorce. In the seven years since we formed FRN, we have collected information from professionals, attorneys, policymakers, psychologists, physicians, politicians and, last but definitely not least, fathers and mothers who have important messages to share with others about divorce, fathers' responsibilities, childrearing, shared custody, and collaboration with an ex-spouse. FRN has let me bring my personal journey full circle, by doing my own part to give back something to my family and the greater community.

This book is full of 20/20 hindsight—hindsight that I hope can help you manage, and minimize, the tumult of divorce, from the early stages of single fatherhood up through and including remarriage and blending families. You'll discover a path that will allow you to keep your kids in your life and create a healthy extended family environment, guided by principles of collaboration and cooperation.

If your first reaction is that your ex will never participate in a collaborative approach to divorce and coparenting, put that out of your mind. Focus on what you can do. This book offers concrete tips, gleaned from my own experiences and the experiences of thousands who have viewed and written the Father.com website. The skills and tools here are designed for fathers, but my intention is to create common ground, and my hope is that the book will be meaningful and helpful to mothers too.

You will not find a lot of theory here. In the midst of a divorce, few of us want to wade through abstraction and ideology. Other books can provide that if you want it. What I hope to provide is a down-to-earth, nuts-and-bolts approach for getting through this difficult period with as few wounds as possible, and for putting good ideas into action right now.

Getting Started

During the very difficult, conflicted early months of divorce, your life can feel like a train wreck, with no relief in sight. It is during those months that the inner disciplines of collaboration and cooperation can pull you through. It's important to maintain perspective in this period of your divorce, realizing that there are many years ahead when things—from raising your children to communicating with your ex—will calm down. You and your children's mom will need support and consideration from each other, and these will be much easier to give and receive if you have been able to hold the intent of cooperation and collaboration from the start.

If you're in the initial stages of a divorce, the prospect of figuring out how to continue sharing the responsibilities of parenting with your soon-to-be ex-wife might be daunting. Yet you also know that your children need the love and guidance of both parents, so for your kids' sake you're determined to get over your own issues with their mother. The stories, insights, and suggestions in this book offer ideas and hope that should help you to meet not only the basic responsibilities of parenting, but also experience the great joys of having children in your life.

You can't wholly shield your children from the pain and trauma of divorce, but there are tried-and-true ways of softening the impact of the transition. Even if your spouse is not cooperative and collaborative—particularly in the first months after the divorce—you can still unilaterally create an environment that minimizes stress and confusion for the kids and provides security for them during the transition. At the very least, your early efforts to act in the most collaborative way possible should plant the seeds of greater cooperation between you and the children's mother in the future.

It's All About the Kids

Children are best served when they have full and open access to both parents and feel they are living in a loving environment, even though Mom and Dad no longer live together. Whether your children live with you full-time, part-time, or not at all, it's important for their stability and well-being that you step up to your role as a responsible, accountable, and compassionate parent. That role begins with helping to guide the family through the unsettling passage that begins the day one parent leaves the family home.

I hope this book will help you navigate these troubled waters with as little damage and as much dignity and compassion as possible, by giving you:

- tips on creating—either unilaterally or with the participation of your children's mother—an environment in which there is room to collaborate on issues involving your children, so they feel part of a loving and nurturing family

- support and encouragement to be the best father you can be: present and accountable, loving and leading, competent and caring
- step-by-step practical guidelines for dealing with day-to-day issues and stresses during and after divorce
- strategies and solutions for collaborative parenting that honor the needs of all members of your extended family, creating common ground and making room for some healing to take place between you and your ex, and
- ideas about how to minimize and deal with the feelings of abandonment and loss of self-esteem that people commonly experience during divorce.

My hope is that this book will help you find your way to a peaceful resolution of your divorce, so that you can ultimately settle down to the creative, rewarding, and pleasurable work of creating your new extended family. ●

with each argument. Finally they were sleeping in different rooms, and Tim sought every opportunity for out-of-town business trips. Gina noticed she was relieved and more relaxed when Tim was out of town and she avoided intimate contact when he was home.

Tim and Gina both felt very alone in their marriage, and were depressed and anxious over the loss of the mutual support they'd once experienced. It was nearly impossible for either of them to accept the fact that something that started so beautifully had come to this.

The children, now five and seven, were beginning to show the effects of the constant tension between their parents. In family counseling, Gina and Tim struggled through the challenges of their own conflicts. In the beginning, they pledged to stay together and resolve their differences. Somehow, they'd make the marriage work. Above all, they both understood the negative impact their separation would have on the kids, and they wanted to avoid this at all costs—well, nearly all costs.

It all came to a head at Alexia's soccer game, when Tim and Gina started arguing in front of the kids and other parents. Deeply humiliated by their own behavior, and aware of how they'd also humiliated their children, they apologized to the people around them and made their way home. Although they were still furious with each other, they made a pact that evening never again to air their conflicts in public. And they would try their best not to argue in front of the kids.

But the conflicts persisted, and the tension continued to affect Alexia and Ben. At last, after much soul-searching and many tears, Tim and Gina looked at each other across their therapist's office one morning and made the decision to end their marriage. It was the first thing they'd agreed on in months. They also made a pledge, suggested by their counselor, to make the break with a specific goal in mind: to do everything in their power to treat one another with respect and dignity. With two beautiful children, they had much to be grateful for. The marriage had blessed them in this way regardless of the fact that they could no longer live together. The therapist assured them that she would be available to help them through the separation, guiding them through what she called "collaborative divorce."

Tim and Gina met while they were both on vacation in Southern California. Tim had just received a dream promotion at his first serious job. Now manager of the marketing department at Quantum, he was riding high and confident of his future. Gina, however, was just coming out of a painful breakup with the young man she'd been dating for two years and was feeling like many things were up in the air for her.

Gina certainly wasn't looking for a new relationship. She welcomed Tim's company but made it clear that she was only interested in having someone to pal around with. Tim said okay, though he was absolutely certain he'd found the love of his life. He'd take his time and give her whatever space she needed. He believed that if he was patient and played his cards right, everything would work out.

> *Divorce is one of the loneliest of modern rituals.*
> —SUZANNE GORDON

Tim's caring attention was exactly what Gina needed to help her through this difficult time. And after several months of telephone conversations across the miles—she lived in Tucson, he in Seattle—they agreed to meet in San Francisco over Labor Day weekend. Gina was ready to give love another chance.

The weekend in San Francisco couldn't have been more perfect. Six months later they were making wedding plans. Gina wanted a traditional church wedding, which was fine with Tim as long as they could have a large reception at a place near the ocean, with all their friends celebrating with them. This was one marriage, they told their friends, that would last forever.

In fact, it lasted for nine and a half years, long enough for Alexia and Ben to be born. Neither Gina nor Tim could remember when the arguments actually started. They were over small things at first, but soon even the small disagreements were turning into major fights. They kissed and made up time after time. It seemed that no matter what one of them suggested to the other, it was steel on flint. Sparks flew, whether the discussion was what to fix for dinner, what to plant in the garden, where to spend their vacation, or how best to discipline the kids. The loving intimacy they'd shared eroded

WARNING

By "collaborative divorce," the therapist meant a way that divorcing parties can relate to each other starting from an assumption of collaboration rather than conflict. In the legal field, there is also a growing movement called "collaborative divorce," which refers to a specific way of going through a legal divorce, in which both parties and their lawyers agree to keep the matter out of court. In this book, the term means a way of relating to your spouse during a divorce, not to the legal process.

You probably recognize Tim and Gina's story. Every marriage is different, and so is every divorce—but the common thread for divorcing parents with children is the need to come to terms with the ongoing relationship you'll have as divorced parents. This book is about that relationship, and about how you can move through the divorce with a commitment to being the best ex-husband and the best divorced father you can be.

One Last Try

Maybe, just maybe, you're not quite ready to call it quits. You're talking about breaking up, and perhaps you've gone through a few periods of reconciliation, but you haven't signed any papers or made any property agreements. Is it worth trying once more? If you think it might be possible to save your marriage, now is the time to try, before one of you moves out. Once you have stepped over that particular threshold, your chances of getting back together are diminished. It's a big step and one that is not easily reversed.

Let's say you're still sharing the same house, however tension-filled it might be. Is it worth it to try counseling? If you're not in counseling already, and you are sincere about giving the marriage one last try, then you should seriously consider asking a third party for help. Let your wife know that you would very much like to enter counseling because you want to stay married to her. Bear in mind, however, that while professional help can be a great asset, it will help save your marriage only if you and your spouse are equally committed to working it out and you both want to keep your marriage intact. That means you want to stay together no matter how uncomfortable the changes you are facing might be—including the need for you to accept your wife's shortcomings and to ask her to accept yours.

DOES COUNSELING MAKE SENSE IF YOU KNOW YOU'RE SPLITTING UP?

Counseling is absolutely worth trying when your goal is to save your marriage, but it can also be worthwhile if you know you're splitting up. A counselor can help you work out how you want to communicate during your separation and after your divorce, especially as your communication relates to parenting your kids together. A counselor can also help you make some of the nitty-gritty decisions about your separation—who will move out of the house, how you will pay for the expenses of two households while you work out a formal agreement, and how you will deal with the kids about the divorce.

People have shared many stories with me about how counseling helped them through breakups. For example, in a group for recently divorced fathers, one man confessed, "My wife had to drag me into counseling kicking and screaming. I made some effort to participate but I was never really into it. I knew our marriage was over, and I wanted out more than I've ever wanted anything in my life. Looking back on it, though, I'm really glad I went. It helped both of us work through some of the fears we had about ending it, and we were able to actually help each other in the separation. Today, we're good friends. We've been able to cooperate really well where the kids are concerned, and that's something both of us consider valuable. I don't think we could have gotten to this place as fast as we did had it not been for those last sessions with the shrink."

Will you be plagued with doubts along the way? Of course. In the haunting hours between midnight and 3 a.m., who does not fall prey to the ghosts of perplexity and skepticism? If you find your doubts and fears keeping you awake at night or distracting you during the day, you might want to consider private therapy, just for you, in addition to any work you are doing as a couple with a marriage counselor. (There's more about counseling below and in Chapter 8.)

Because separating can be so complicated and frightening, many couples go through a trial separation before making their final decision. By the time a couple has gotten to the point of choosing to live apart, it's likely that they'll eventually go on to make the separation permanent. But once in a great while, given some time apart, a couple will get a better perspective on what it would really mean to be divorced. That may lead them to accept shared responsibility for creating the current estrangement and develop the motivation to work a little harder to get back together.

A trial separation can be difficult where the kids are concerned, however. What do you tell them? Do you say, "Dad (or maybe Mom) is going to have a place of his own for a while, but don't worry, we'll be getting back together?" Given that you can't actually promise your kids that you'll reconcile, better to offer them something solid they can deal with. Just assure them that "Even though Dad is going to have a place of his own now, he's still your dad, and he'll always be your dad. You'll still see a lot of him, and you'll also have another home where you can go to be with him." Assuring the kids that while things are changing, Dad will always be Dad helps them deal with their primary fear—that you won't love them anymore.

If you decide to try a separation period, be sure that you jointly decide how long the separation will be. Between six and twelve months is reasonable. But be specific. Both of you should agree on a date. After that time, you can take a look at your situation—perhaps with the help of your marriage counselor or therapist—and then decide what your next move is going to be.

If this is to be a trial separation, make sure you're in agreement about what this means: you are still married to each other, and your goal is to get back together. If you get emotionally and sexually involved with another person, it's no longer a trial separation. If that's happened already and is a part of why you're separating, you need to end that "other" relationship so that you can focus on your marriage. It's important to remember that even after the divorce is final, most of us feel some pangs of sadness, or perhaps even anger, when we see our ex-partner with someone else. Time does heal such wounds, but if you're sincere about a trial separation you'll realize, early on, that this is not a time to open up new wounds. Instead it is a time to heal the wounds that are threatening your marriage.

It is virtually impossible to know with absolute certainty that separating from your partner is the right way to go, even after you've tried every other option. What you do know is that you are in pain, and your wife is in pain, and your children are in pain and may be showing the stresses of your struggle. If you've reached the point where you feel there's no other option but to separate permanently, you're about to find out that you are not alone on the journey, no matter how much it might feel like that sometimes. Everyone in the immediate family is affected, to say nothing of grandparents, friends, and even distant cousins. While that might feel like a lot of pressure, it should also support your commitment to a collaborative process that won't drag those friends and relatives into your conflicts with your spouse.

Honoring the Bonds of Our Children

One evening in a men's divorce group, one of the men was commemorating the third year of his separation from his ex-wife. He reflected on the most difficult parts of the separation and divorce, and reiterated how relieved he was to be out of the marriage. He then made this comment: "In the beginning there are those little moments of grace when you think how mellow it is to be out of this hassle. No more arguments. No more impossible standoffs you know are futile. And then, maybe a couple months out of the house, you start to realize that as long as you live you'll be a part of this family unit, by virtue of the fact of your children. For the first time in my life I know what they mean by that saying, blood is thicker than water."

In so many ways, divorce—at least when there are children of the marriage—is not ending a relationship but changing that relationship. Where children are concerned, Dad is still Dad and Mom is still Mom. There may be stepparents who at least partially take on those roles, and who your children may even come to call Dad, but the reality is that the bonds you share with your children do not go away. Keeping that in mind, look for ways to honor those bonds even as you are making plans to leave the marriage.

True Stories: Keep Your Eyes on the Prize

A friend recently shared with me an experience he'd had at his daughter's wedding, 12 years after he and her mother divorced. Before the wedding, he and his ex-wife spoke on the phone, promising each other that while they were both attending the wedding there would be no scenes between them. This was a time of celebration, not a time for opening old wounds. What surprised my friend, he said, was that when the band started playing at the reception, he had a profound yearning to dance with his ex. When he timidly walked up to her to ask, she smiled brightly and eagerly drew him out onto the dance floor. Later she said, "I was so afraid you wouldn't ask me." It was not anything like a reconciliation, he said, for they had both gone on with their lives and remarried. But clearly, they shared a bond through their daughter, and it felt good to acknowledge and celebrate it in this way. "I am so glad we were able to share this moment," my friend told his former wife.

This man's clear perspective is a valuable insight for all of us—that where there are children involved, there is a bond that we will share with our kids' moms forever. After the divorce, we're still going to be raising the children together with our former spouses, and this will take a collaborative effort if we're to do it right. In the ideal world, of course, there would be no domestic strife and no divorce. But that's not what this book is about. Living as we do in a world where divorce is all too prevalent, we would do well to look at the best ways through it—beginning with the realization that a family with children is a family that is bonded together for many, many years to come. But that's the big picture. In the moment, you're first going to have to tell the kids about the impending divorce.

CALLING A TRUCE

This is a big one. You still have many unresolved differences between you. You may be feeling raw and hurt. Even so, once you've made the decision to divorce, there's business to attend to, some of which is going to require strength that you may have never imagined you possess. You've got to step back, survey what needs to be done, and then move on to complete what you've set into motion. This is where true collaboration begins, with an agreement to call a truce: an end to active fighting. This book will help you keep your commitment to that collaboration.

Your first purpose in calling a truce is to be able to sit down with the kids and tell them what's going on. This is not about you or how you feel; it is about your kids. This moment will stay with them forever, so be prepared to put your hurt and anger aside and focus on what they need.

There are other reasons to call a truce with your spouse, though. The stress of continual conflict, as you already know, takes its toll. Now that you have decided to split, you have an opportunity to relieve some of that stress by agreeing to deal with each other in a collaborative way. Doing so will make everything easier, from arranging a visitation schedule to splitting your bank accounts. There is no way around it—this is a very hard time for everyone. There's no need to make it harder by fighting over every little detail.

In the ideal world, Mom and Dad would sit down with the kids and in an orderly, compassionate, and age-appropriate way, tell them what was going on. However, at this point, usually one or both of you is feeling anxious and confused, and talking to the kids in a healthy and useful way feels impossible. Still, no matter how you feel, you're simply going to have to pull yourself together and move forward with this difficult task. There is no easy way to do this. Just do your best, and when in doubt, bet on the truth.

It's best for the kids if you and your spouse talk to them at the same time—but make certain you agree to this ahead of time and talk over how it's going to go. If you're feeling very unsure, seek help from a marriage counselor. This can greatly reduce your anxiety by giving you some guidelines to follow. For example, if your kids are very different ages, you'll need to speak to each of them in a way that will make sense to them. For example, a four-year old child may only need to hear three things, though you may have to repeat these three statements many times in the weeks ahead: 1) "I love you," 2) "I will always be your daddy," and 3) "I am going to be living in a different house where you will have your own room and toys, just like here." Telling a teenager may be more challenging. The main thing with teenagers will be to keep focused while avoiding discussions that are critical of their mother. If you have doubts about how to present this information to your kids, a counselor can help you understand where your kids are developmentally and how to talk to each of them.

Whatever you do, after you explain to the kids about the changes that are about to happen, make sure you take each child aside separately and address each child's individual concerns and needs one on one. Encourage them to ask questions and to express what they are feeling. Answer their questions without putting down their mother in any way. And take the time to acknowledge their feelings without dissecting them or trying to talk them out of it. For example, if your daughter tells you she is "sad and angry and scared all at the same time," let her know that you understand why she would feel that way, that she may feel that way for a while, and that it will get better.

If she's angry at you, you might say "I'm sure you are angry, sweetheart. I'm sorry that you feel this way and I understand why you do right now. I believe that you'll feel better as time goes on, but it might take a while. I still love you very much, and that will never change."

True Stories: A Cautionary Tale

When my wife and I split up, we told each of our three kids at different times and places. We did not make a lot of time for them to express their reactions or ask questions, which was a mistake. My eight-year-old son was especially confused by the way we told him. Both his mom and I held him in our laps in such a loving way that he thought something wonderful was about to happen. When we explained that his mom and I were getting a divorce, it didn't make sense to him. He couldn't put together the loving nurturing and the shocking news of the divorce. It was a lack of planning on our part, and a failure to consider what message our actions might send, that caused his confusion and meant we had to backtrack and start over dealing with his feelings. On the other hand, we tried not to get too down on ourselves—we did the best we could in the moment, and there's no perfect way to break news like this. Most kids are going to need ongoing help in coping with the divorce, no matter how well the initial conversation goes.

Regardless of how you choose to tell your kids, do so in a way that is sensitive to their individual needs, in an age-appropriate manner, with your actions and words expressing a coherent message. There's no way to avoid some upset—yours and theirs. Be as aware as you possibly can of your children's reactions. The more you are able to observe how they are taking the news, the better able you'll be to handle any difficulties they may be having, now and in the future.

Tell Them You Love Them, and Tell Them Often

As much as you want to ease your kids' and your own pain at this point, there really is nothing you can do to rush the healing that must take place. It's here that the old Taoist saying, "Don't push the river," becomes the rule of the day. But while healing takes time, there are things you can say that will help your kids through the transition, keeping them in a place of relative safety as they negotiate this new territory. Here are key concepts that you'll want to convey to your kids. Don't drag out your discussion of these points—keep your communication clear, simple, and age-appropriate:

- Assure them the divorce is not their fault and that they are not in any way responsible for Mom and Dad wanting to live in different houses.
- Tell them you're sorry to have caused this mess.
- Assure them that even though you may not be living in the same house with them, you will not ever abandon them—you are all still a family, and that will never change.
- Ask them to be patient and tell them that many other kids have gone through this—and that eventually it will get easier and they will feel "normal" again.
- Tell them often that you love them.

True Stories: Acting Out the Teenage Ways

When Jerry and Brenda broke up, their oldest son, Craig, then fourteen, acted out by cutting school and getting involved with a group of kids who were experimenting with drugs. Jerry had the boy come and live with him for a period of time in the hope of getting him away from the kids he was hanging out with. "It was hellish," Jerry said. "Craig lied constantly, stole from me, and eventually got suspended from school.

"One day a cop came to the door and reported that my son was selling weed. We were subpoenaed to appear for a hearing with a juvenile probation officer. That meeting scared the crap out of both of us. When we got home afterwards, I asked Craig what it was that bothered him so much. His first answer was that I bugged him, and he hated my guts. Then he broke down and sobbed, 'I don't have a family anymore.'

"I contacted a family therapist the next day. What came out in our meeting with the therapist was a great revelation to both Craig and me: we learned that, regardless of the divorce, we were still a family. My ex and I had not destroyed that family by breaking up, but we had forced it to change its form.

"For several weeks, Craig and I and our counselor worked together to decide ways our new family structure might work. To make a long story short, Craig chose to go back and live with his Mom and my other two kids. His acting out has stopped and he's taken a very caring and responsible role with his younger siblings. I'm really proud for both of us because I think we got to the bottom of a pretty big problem that might otherwise have been a real tragedy."

Decide to Be the Best Dad You Can Be

Dissolving a marriage, particularly when children are involved, is a complex and trying process. It's hard on everyone. As one recently divorced father put it, "It is like having the cosmic carpet pulled suddenly from under your feet. Even though I thought I was prepared for it, and had done a lot in therapy around it, when I walked out that door for the last time, I felt like the earth had crumbled under my feet."

During this period of transition, you'll no doubt encounter a great deal of confusion and emotional upheaval. You'll probably be feeling every emotion imaginable, running the spectrum from anger and fear to relief to deep sadness. All that being so, hold the intention uppermost in your mind that regardless of what else is going on, you'll do everything you can to be the best father that you can possibly be. If you make and keep that commitment to yourself, you may encounter trials of many kinds, but you will find a way to keep your kids' mental, emotional, spiritual, and physical health at the top of your priority list.

What does this mean in a practical sense? It means that you put your kids' needs before your own—a theme that we'll return to again and again in this book. It means that you pay attention to what your kids are saying and what they're doing—both with you and with their friends, at school, and with your spouse. It means that no matter how stressed out, overwhelmed, or burned out you feel, you find a way to show up for your kids—not just when they are in crisis or acting out, but when it's time to help with the homework or drive the carpool on any given day.

If you can do this, you'll receive two enormous benefits. First, you'll improve your relationship with your kids and offer them the support that they need. And second, you'll undoubtedly improve your own emotional state. Focusing on something other than your own problems will help you heal and move on.

True Stories: Brent Learns to be a Parent

Brent, whose daughter was five years old when he divorced her mother, told the story of how, soon after leaving the family home and finding an apartment for himself, he felt literally overcome by anxiety and depression. The first time he was supposed to have little Shelly for the weekend, he called up and cancelled. "I just couldn't do it," he said. "I was a total basket case." In his own mind, he was a big failure as a dad, and his first reaction was to just withdraw entirely from his daughter's life.

"Fortunately," he said. "I had a friend who'd been through a similar thing. She told me not to beat myself up for not seeing Shelly that weekend. I should still hold my intention and do my level best to get myself together."

Brent did exactly that, and unless he was out of town on business, he kept his weekend visits with his daughter. Ultimately, he did become the kind of father he wanted to be—present, available, consistent— and while there were difficulties over the years he was able to keep a loving and caring focus with her.

Taking Care of Yourself

Many couples find it very useful, in the early part of the divorce, to get help from a marriage counselor. The counselor will be offering not marriage counseling but collaborative divorce counseling. The counselor may work with the two of you together, or may be your own individual therapist. If you and your spouse do see someone together, you may also want to get some professional support just for you.

Finding your way to a collaborative divorce depends on your ability to recognize when it's okay to go it alone and when you can use experienced help. Above all, don't be the victim of false pride. It's not always easy to ask for help, whether it's about the best way to get from point A to point B, or how to best handle personal matters. Try to resist the *I can do this myself* approach. At this stage of the journey, you're best off looking for the shortest and easiest route through the divorce process, the one that will inflict minimal damage upon everyone involved. Getting help will usually support that effort. After all, if you had been able to sort out your problems on your own, you would not now be divorcing. This is not a judgment of you or your spouse, by the way. Every one of us is unique, and when we put two or more people together, their differences can either complicate communication or make it easier. In a divorce, the issue is nearly always the former.

Experienced professionals have helped others through the process many times and can ease you through it. Having an unbiased third party involved will make communication with your spouse much easier, increasing your ability to resolve issues together.

Through all of it, it's important to stay focused. Your goal is to learn a way of relating to your soon-to-be ex-spouse that will be healthy for your kids. You are not in therapy to get back together with your spouse. Yes, it does happen now and then, but don't confuse your own counseling with couples therapy. What you are doing here is resolving your own core issues that will have serious long-term effects on your children and their mother.

There are lots of other ways that you can take care of yourself, including the old standbys of eating right, exercising, and getting enough sleep. Make sure you do whatever works for you, whether it's daily meditation or joining a softball league.

WHAT ARE FRIENDS FOR?

In times of crisis, most of us seek out the comfort and solace of our friends. In the beginning, you may be very angry, looking for ways to justify what's happened to your marriage. You need the support of friends and family at this time, but be careful not to abuse their willingness to listen. Family members need to be told, of course, but they don't need an itemized account of your grievances. As one man told me, "I look back on the period of my divorce with genuine regret. What happened is that I not only lost my marriage but a couple of good friendships I really valued. I never should have burdened them with my rants—and believe me, I really did rant."

Divorce is a touchy subject for nearly everyone. Even the best relationships have a few sharp edges. Your stories can open old wounds, or create new ones, with the friends you share them with. So no matter how much you may want to transform the sour feelings that are lodged in your heart, take a moment to consider how helping you with that work will impact your friend.

Who Moves Out?

In most cases, it's the father who moves out of the family home. The main reason for this is to minimize the disruption in the children's lives, assuming that Mom is the primary caregiver. From the kids' point of view, it is painful to have a parent move out, so make sure that regardless of who leaves the house, you maintain the home base that gives the kids a sense of familiarity and security. This is not always possible, of course. Families may have to downsize to a smaller home or move to another neighborhood or city. But whatever life necessitates, don't ever lose sight of how important it is for children to have the security of a place that feels like home.

If you're the one who moves out, you'll have to deal with the kids' perception that you are the one ending the marriage. The reality is that the children don't need to know who ended the marriage. Placing blame won't bring them any peace of mind, and will tend to create a conflict that can never be fully resolved. Older children might ask you who is to blame, of course. What should you answer? Simply explain that there are situations in life when who's to blame really isn't the issue, and that both of you had your part in causing the deterioration of your relationship.

What else should you discuss with them? The kids don't need to know the gory details of what goes on in private between you and your spouse. Most parents' first reflex will be to spare the kids the details of the divorce, which is appropriate. Never discuss with them anything about your sexual relationship or other truly adult concerns.

There's no point lying to your kids about what's been going on—they were there. Even children who appear to only have the most rudimentary grasp of language can often determine what's the truth and what's not. Young children won't understand the same issues as the older kids, of course, so you need to gear your conversations with them so that they can grasp what's happening. And very small kids—infants and toddlers who aren't yet really talking—don't have the language skills for whatever you tell them to make much sense. Still, give them age-appropriate information if and when they do start asking.

If there has been a lot of tension between you and your spouse, the kids will have experienced it too. And obviously, if there have been other overt problems, such as emotional or physical violence, mental illness, or drug or alcohol abuse, the kids will likely already be aware of this too, no matter what their ages. Kids often feel great relief when the tension is relieved once one parent moves out. That relief needs to be acknowledged along with all of their other feelings.

And don't put down your spouse in any way. If you're very angry, this may cut down on how much you can talk to your kids about their other parent, but it will be well worth it in the long run. Negative talk about your ex will make your kids feel that they're caught in the middle. They'll be learning a lesson of resentment and anger, rather than one of compassion and patience. And they'll see you as someone who's harsh and unforgiving, which is likely to alienate them from you. In short, there's no benefit and a lot of downside to trashing your ex to your kids or in their presence.

True Stories: Kids' Feelings

"I thought my kids were taking the whole thing pretty well," Don told the men's group one evening. "Dianna, my daughter, who's eight, even told me, 'you'll always be my Daddy, forever.' I believed she understood everything I was telling her. But when I went back to pick her up for the weekend, she wouldn't say a word to me. She just sulked the whole weekend."

Many divorced parents have this experience. No matter how understanding and mature your kids may seem to be, your leaving will cause them to feel abandoned and angry. They'll probably also feel ambivalent as they try to reconcile their anger with the love for you and the sense of permanence that you represent in their lives.

No matter what their ages and levels of maturity, you can count on the kids reacting in a variety of different ways—sometimes all within a matter of minutes. They are providing you with the information you'll need over the next few months to deal with the transitions you are all going through. Here is a list of just some of the feelings you might expect to hear about:

- relief to be free from witnessing fighting and arguments
- withdrawal and disbelief
- shock
- worry about how their lives will change (one friend who was 5 or 6 when her parents divorced said her first thought was "Who will put me to bed?")
- anger at one or both parents, especially the parent who is leaving the family home
- blame towards either parent, but especially the one who is leaving the family home
- shame and embarrassment
- confusion about loyalty to one or other parent
- bewilderment about who to believe when the parents disagree, and
- guilt—believing they may be to blame for the breakup.

Be prepared and know that the best medicine at this time is to support them in acknowledging and sharing their feelings, regardless of what they might be.

Your kids' difficult reactions don't mean that you should rethink the divorce or consider going back to the family home to assuage their feelings. What it does mean is that you need to listen very carefully to their complaints and their silences as well. Their sense of security, which is so important at this stage of the divorce, will depend on your ability to listen and to let them know that you accept their feelings.

Leave the Lawyer Stuff for Later if You Can

When they first split up, many people believe they must immediately seek out an attorney and file for divorce. For some people, starting the legal process is the way to reduce the confusing feelings and feel some relief. For others, it's necessary to file right away because of support or custody issues. But it's not necessary for everyone. Here are some factors to consider.

- If you have young children and you and your spouse can't agree about how you will divide time with them or pay for their support, you'll need to get some temporary orders from a court right away. This requires that one of you file the papers to start the divorce.

- If you can't agree who will move out of the home, you'll also have to get a court to decide that, meaning that someone will have to file papers.

- If you can agree on who moves out, an amount of temporary support, and how you will share time with the kids, then you can hold off on starting the legal proceedings.

- If you have reasons to stay legally married, such as wanting to keep insurance in force for your wife and kids as long as possible, you can also wait to file until some time has passed.

- Your divorce won't be final for quite a while after it's filed. States have different rules on this but in most states, there's a waiting period of 6 to 12 months. So if you have some reason to want the divorce to be finalized promptly—such as that you want to get married again—you'll need to file soon.

It's definitely true that while you and your soon-to-be ex are still volatile emotionally—which is normal—you should not be trying to make any big decisions. Wait until you start to feel more solid. If you can hold off on filing for a while, fine. But no matter what, consider getting an hour's consultation with an attorney so that you can ask whatever questions you have. Here's a brief list of things you may want to know right away—and there's more about dealing with lawyers in Chapter 6:

- Custody rights: what's customary? What is possible given any special circumstances you might have, such as your moving to another city or another state, or your spouse's desire to relocate?
- How will the marital property be divided and who will be responsible for debts?
- How much might you be required to pay to your spouse as child support? What about alimony?
- How will the divorce affect your taxes?

You may be able to calculate, on the basis of this meeting, how the divorce is going to affect your finances. In this way you'll be able to estimate how much money you'll have available for the rent and other additional expenses you'll be having. You may also be able to set your mind at rest about whatever worries you're having about seeing your kids.

Money, Money, Money, Money

Money is a major issue in most divorces—just as it is in most marriages. If you're a two-income family, the burden will be a bit easier to handle because in most cases, you'll be sharing the expenses. If you are the main breadwinner, you'll have to start supporting two households—yours and hers. Clearly, this can be a major financial burden, one that may necessitate some big changes in your lifestyle. This alone may stir up feelings of frustration, anxiety, and anger.

This is the point at which many men withdraw because they feel overwhelmed by their feelings and by the changes in their family structure. Some even abandon their fathering responsibilities. As much as it might seem that you need to cut and run, hang on. Don't bail out on your responsibilities to your family. Sure, you're going to have to do some belt-tightening. And, yes, you may feel resentful if your ex stays in the house and gets to spend more time with the kids and it seems that she has a much nicer life that you have to pay for. Just keep in mind that the home she's living in is also providing shelter and security for your children; the sacrifices you're going to be making are for their benefit. It's also statistically true that for many women, divorce is financially disastrous. Your spouse is probably panicked about how she is going to afford to live and help to support the kids in the long run. The big house may feel more like a burden than a blessing at this transition point. And she's just as emotionally raw as you are about the divorce and the money issues involved. So try to cut her a break wherever you can.

Financial worries can be frightening and distracting. But once again, you'll need to remind yourself to keep your kids on the top of your priority list. Be available to them emotionally. Show up for them a hundred percent.

MONEY AND CONTROL AS A SUBSTITUTE FOR RELATIONSHIP

One of the biggest shocks that men face in the first months of their divorce is how radically their relationship changes with their ex. Suddenly money becomes the main focus of virtually every interaction between you. This is especially true if you have been the major breadwinner and will now be supporting two households. After a while, you'll wonder what happened to the person you once loved and who loved you. Why is it now only about the bucks?

And what about her? She'll be amazed at your seeming indifference to her financial needs. (And if your spouse has been the breadwinner, you'll probably feel the same, in addition to whatever feelings you have about asking her to continue supporting you.) There's a great distance between you now, maybe even a wall that neither of you can scale. One divorcing father admitted after he and his wife spent years working in couples' therapy, only to conclude that they couldn't save their marriage: "I miss part of what we had always shared and can hardly believe the way money has become the only thing we ever discuss anymore...with every exchange between us turning into a power struggle."

To get past that, you can't sink into self-pity, revenge, and victimization. What divorcing couples find, and what you will have to accept, is that divorcing and living apart create perhaps as many demands as being together—and when it comes to finances, even more demands.

RESOURCES

Whether or not you hire a lawyer, make sure you get informed. There are lots of useful divorce resources out there, including:

Divorce & Money: How to Make the Best Financial Decisions During Divorce, by Violet Woodhouse with Dale Fetherling (Nolo). Practical and proactive advice to help you protect yourself and safeguard your financial future. Reduces the financial complications of divorce into comprehensible strategies

The Complete Guide to Protecting Your Financial Security When Getting a Divorce, by Alan Feigenbaum (McGraw-Hill). Arms readers with the knowledge and tools they need to make it through a divorce with their financial skins intact.

Divorce and Money: Everything You Need to Know, by Gayle Rosenwald Smith (Perigee Books). Explains the financial issues involved in divorce and, most important, tells the reader what they can do to better understand their situation and how to take proper action.

Hang In There

You are at the beginning of a journey that may very well bring you face to face with some very difficult feelings, including resentment, anger, sadness, and anxiety. Have faith, however, that there is a way through these challenges. You'll find, in the pages to come, a compilation of the experiences of many other men who have traveled this path before you and who have not only survived the difficult times but have come to a place of peace. Some have even come full circle to enjoy amicable relationships with their ex-wives. Trust that things will get easier over time. All you can do is hang in there and put one foot in front of the other—and read on! ●

Creating Your New Home

The decision has been made. You and your wife are going to separate. You may not be the one who initiated this parting of the ways, but you are very likely to be the person who leaves the family home. You might be looking forward to finally having some relief from the constant tension you've been experiencing for so long. But there are some tough realities to face as well. At the top of the list is the fact that, along with being separated from your wife, you're also going to be separated from your children. You'll be seeing them, of course, but from now on it may be mostly short visits—weekends, holidays, special occasions, and perhaps some regular school days. You will want to stay in touch, visit often, and have them stay with you in your home, but chances are even telephone calls back and forth will have to be arranged ahead of time.

> *Start by doing what's necessary; then do what's possible; and suddenly you are doing the impossible*
>
> —ST. FRANCIS OF ASSISI

Most men who've been close to their kids find the first several months away from the family home filled with heartache and a sense of loss. You may find yourself in a constant debate with yourself: *Have I done the right thing? Have I missed something important here, something I might still be able to address with my ex? Will I lose the kids' love? What if my ex remarries and the kids get along really well with their stepdad and ditch me? What are the kids thinking and feeling about me these days?*

Whatever else is going through your mind, your main concern needs to be how your kids are doing. The more you focus on them and their needs, the more you'll come into alignment with what's important and necessary. At the same time, at this highly emotional time, there may be times when you scream at your ex, slam down the phone when she calls, storm around the house pissed off and totally losing sight of the kids' needs. Don't give yourself a bad time about it. You're only human. Just keep coming back to center, turning your healthy focus back to the kids' needs—and setting your sights on the ultimate goal of establishing a collaborative relationship with your ex.

The conflicts kids experience in divorce can be quite complicated, and it's important to know a little about the kinds of issues and anxieties they face. Here are some of the big ones:

- Adjusting to the fact that Dad doesn't live with them anymore.
- Being angry with Dad for abandoning them—even though this might not be the case.
- Being angry with Dad because, "he must be the bad guy, he had to go away."
- Blaming themselves for the breakup.
- Adjusting to having two homes—one with Mom, one with Dad.
- Fearing that since Dad abandoned them, how can they be sure Mom won't go too?
- Finding it difficult to be around either parent if that parent is always talking about how heartbroken he or she is over the other wanting a divorce. (Makes kids feel they have to take sides.)

This constitutes only a very short sample of the many ways that kids may be affected by divorce. I've listed these because they are ones that as adults we might not even consider. For example, because you're so close to the real issues you had with your ex, it might never occur to you that your son or daughter might see himself or herself as the cause of your breakup. Similarly, it might never enter your mind that your kids would feel you had deliberately abandoned them. After all, you still talk to them on the phone several times a week, attend all their games, and see them at least on weekends. Where's the abandonment? However, with all of that they can still feel like you've walked out on their lives.

Likewise it may seem to you that it's obvious you're all better off with you and your spouse living separately—no more conflict and tension at home. But to your kids, the family as they know it may be the most important thing, and they may continue to fantasize that you and their mom will get back together again.

Making a Home

First things first. You've got to have a place where your kids can feel at home, and that means making your new place feel like home to you. This may very well be a challenge because you're probably downsizing, and you're likely to be living in a more modest place than your ex and the kids are. If you're living in a smaller place in a neighborhood that's not as nice, it may take a while for both you and your kids to adjust. Older children, in particular, can be hyper-aware of these differences. Their anger and anxiety about your breakup may come out in the form of them letting you know that you are not living up to their expectations.

True Stories: Mobile Homes Are Home, Too

When Daniel divorced, he purchased a large, three-bedroom mobile home in a decent community at the edge of town. He chose this place not only because he could afford it but also because it offered amenities he thought his daughter might enjoy. There was a swimming pool, a gym, a tennis court, and a small lake less than half a mile away, with sailboats and canoes. It was a tidy, well-kept community, with stunning flower gardens, thanks to a number of retirees living there.

In spite of it all, Ibis, his 14-year-old daughter, was anything but impressed. She refused to stay overnight on her first visit. When Daniel dropped her off at her mother's, she turned to him and said, "I never dreamed my own father would become trailer trash." Daniel was stunned. He drove away feeling shamed and hurt.

But Daniel was patient. He understood that his daughter might be angry at him for a while, that regardless of what she was told to the contrary, she might blame him for the divorce. He also knew that her anger might come out in backhanded ways because it would take her a while to work out what was going on with her.

By the end of the first summer, Ibis had discovered the swimming pool and tennis courts and had enrolled in a sailing class on the lake. Soon she eagerly looked forward to visits with Dad, where there were more things to do than at her Mom's.

It was years before Ibis could tell her dad that in her mind, because he was the one who left the family home, he was to blame for the breakup. She had seen him as the culprit and had looked for ways to put him down. The "trailer trash" comment had been one of the ways she'd found to express her anger.

In her senior year in high school, Ibis thanked her father for all he'd done for her after the divorce. One of the things she named as particularly important during the transition was that he'd given her the master bedroom in his new home, which included her own phone and her own separate bathroom. These were the pinnacles of luxury for a teenage girl. She knew he had spoiled her, though at the time it made her feel that he really cared about her. She knew she would always have a place in his home.

It's the patient dad, the dad who hangs in there, expressing his love, continuing to give his kids the best life he can provide even when they seem totally unappreciative, who finally comes out on top, loved and admired by his kids. It may take more time than you'd like, and you'll have to be careful about setting reasonable limits on their behavior as you guide them through the difficult first months of your divorce. But without this kind of love and caring as the bottom line, the kids can end up in tough shape indeed.

The home you make for yourself and for your kids can go a long way toward resolving many issues for them. If your children feel that they have a secure place with you in your home, and that you are reasonably happy in this new place, modest though it might be, some of their concerns will be ameliorated. But be as attentive as you can to issues that may be troubling them. If you see that your kids are having trouble at school, arguing frequently or intensely with their mother or siblings, showing hostility and aggression toward peers, or demonstrating personality changes, don't hesitate to consult with a therapist who specializes in child development. There's a lot that you can do to help your kids through these difficult times (and there's more about that in Chapter 7).

Ideally, you and your spouse will work together on dealing with issues involving your kids. Make every possible effort to put aside differences you might be having in order to deal with problems your kids may be having. Consider the possibility of family counseling where your kids can meet with a counselor alone or together with you and/or your spouse.

Location, Location, Location

When you move out of your home, you may feel like moving way out, and leaving the stress and complexities far behind. Hovering at the edge of your consciousness may be dreams of escaping to the South Pacific, to Alaska, or to Mars—or at the very least, to the next state over. But as millions of men have discovered, there is no quick escape from the feelings tumbling around in your mind at this time—and you know in your heart that you just can't abandon your kids without making their lives much harder and creating consequences that will one day come back to bite you.

Returning to reality, you realize that if you want to stay involved with your kids, you will have to consider a great number of practical everyday issues. For example, you want to be close to the kids' school, and they will want their home with you in a place where they can still have access to their friends.

Obviously, you can't have your children enrolled in two different schools—one at Mom's house, the other at yours. So make it a priority to find a place where your kids can maintain familiar contacts with friends, teachers, and after-school activities such as classes, clubs, or teams. Kids need the stability of their routines and their friends during this time of transition. Older kids often depend on their friends to talk through problems they're having. While the peer culture of teenagers these days comes with its own set of problems, don't underestimate the positive aspects of your children's connection to their friends. As one man put it, "I would often be in the next room and overhear my daughter Julie talking with her friends on the phone. I couldn't hear the details but there were often tears and even a little raging about things I know Julie wasn't comfortable expressing with her mom and me. Personally, I'm grateful she had friends who encouraged her to vent like that because I think she just needed to get her emotions out there, to have someone her own age listen to her."

And make no mistake: they also need their mom to be easily accessible when they're with you. Whenever possible, kids should have free and open access to both parents and to all other friends and relatives who have played an important part in their lives. Being within walking or biking distance of Mom's house is ideal for the kids. That proximity is certainly going to minimize your need to taxi your kids back and forth. In addition, if you work full time, as most of us do, having your ex's backup can make life much easier for you.

This depends on how well the two of you can collaborate. And for various reasons, this closeness is not always possible or even desirable. Joseph got an apartment just two blocks from his ex's home. Every time his ex needed a babysitter to go out on a date, or simply to go shopping, she called him to help. "At first," he said, "I thought it would be good if I went over to the house and sat with my kids over there. But it was painful. Every time I walked in the front door I was confronted with my memories of the hard times I'd spent there. Then, about three months after we filed for divorce, my ex brought in her new friend to introduce him to me, and that was it. I wasn't ready for that. I just had to stop going over there. Then the kids came to my place, which was just a tiny studio apartment and too cramped for all of us.

Finally I decided I didn't want to be that close to Deborah and see her comings and goings. I moved across town to a new place. It has much more space and a yard where the kids are welcome to play, and there are other kids in the neighborhood. It's not ideal, I suppose, but I'm more comfortable and the kids have their own room, which is good. They actually seem to like it better than our previous arrangement, maybe because it's more like a home for me, too."

You may not have a choice about where you live. Your job or your ex's job may require you to move away—a few miles or across the country—from your kids. Distance complicates spending time with your kids. You'll have to make arrangements for them to visit you, or for you to visit them.

> **TIP**
>
> CONTACT THE KIDS REGULARLY—AT LEAST ONCE OR TWICE A WEEK. If you can afford it, and your kids can be trusted to use it responsibly, consider paying for them to have their own phone.

Regular contact by phone is certainly helpful, but it's not a substitute for actual contact. Budget your time and your money so that you can visit the kids, or have them visit you, as often as humanly possible. Gordon's example below, while not typical, provides some insight into how difficulties such as long distance visits with our kids might be managed in a collaborative divorce, when parents make the kids' well-being their top priority, and build their collaboration on that foundation.

True Stories: A Happy Ending

"When Sylvia and I broke up," said Gordon, "we decided it would work best for everyone concerned if she took a work transfer to Pennsylvania, where her folks live. Grandma would then help out with the after-school childcare while Sylvia was at work. Besides, we both thought the family bonds with our son Andy's grandparents and some of his cousins who lived around there would be a good influence during the transition. I'd been able to stay friends with Sylvia's brother and other members of her family, so every couple of months I could go back there, stay with her brother and sister-in-law, and spend some valuable one-on-one time with Andy. It worked out pretty well, and eventually Sylvia and I were able to manage a much more cooperative relationship, so that when I got an opportunity to move closer to Andy and her—in nearby New Jersey, as a matter of fact—we were all ready for it. That was one of the rewards of being able to work things out together and not have great walls between us just because of our divorce. Andy and I do a lot of things together now, and Sylvia and I have learned to be pretty collaborative where he's concerned."

Gordon and Sylvia's divorce illustrates how important it is for our kids to feel secure and loved even in the midst of a divorce, and how successful coparenting can be when we are able to help our kids feel that way. Mom and Dad both reap the benefits of a good collaboration because the kids are certain in their own minds that they are still loved, in spite of the fact that their parents no longer live together. They still have a family where they feel loved and supported. Gordon and Sylvia's family was not broken—it was extended.

Make Room for the Kids

I have known several men who, faced with the realities of being single again, rented studios or small one-bedroom apartments with great views or particularly desirable locations. It's certainly human enough to want a place with ambience. But where are the kids going to fit in? Sure, they can camp out on your living room floor in their sleeping bags. It might even be fun for them...for a while. Then they'll start getting the message that you really aren't making room for them in your new life.

If you can possibly afford it, your kids should have a room of their own in your home. (And if they are teenagers of different genders, each should have a room.) Can't afford that kind of rent, plus your child support? There are usually ways of working it out, even with limited space. (Remember Daniel's mobile home park?) Use your ingenuity with the goal of making your children feel that you are doing your very best to make a comfortable place for them in your life. Above all, you want to send them the message, through your actions, words, and deeds, that you treasure them and that you put time, energy, and thought into their well-being wherever you are living.

AND WHAT ABOUT MY NEEDS?

While we're on the subject of your creature comforts, what about new people in your life? Most of us want companionship, at the very least. Sometimes that means having a close friend. Sometimes It means having a sexual partner. Sometimes it means we're already looking for a person who will replace the spouse we're divorcing. My advice? Give it time. There's lots more about this in Chapter 10, including advice about how dating can impact the legal aspects of your divorce. For now, just remember to keep your focus on what's best for your children.

Physical and psychological space are both important. Most kids need a certain amount of privacy and need to know that their possessions are safe. If all you can manage is a single closet or a footlocker for your child's belongings, do that. In a small living space, a throw rug and a cabinet or dresser for your child's clothes and toys can give them the sense of privacy and ownership that says, "This is my space. I have a place here, and I want you to respect it." Do, in fact, respect that space as your child's. Make it very clear to your children that this is their space, and have them fully participate in creating it by choosing what they're going to put there and how they want it decorated. Don't make the mistake of absently sticking something of your own there without asking. It may be convenient to use the top drawers of your child's chest of drawers for bills and old checkbook registers, but if that's really the only place you can find for them, be sure you get permission first.

Your creature comforts are important, too, in part because if this place doesn't feel like your home, your children are going to pick that up almost immediately. Whatever house or apartment you choose should be a pleasant place for you, somewhere you'll feel good coming back to every night. Surround yourself with the things that help you to feel connected, creative, and up. Fix the place up so that it pleases you and the kids. Bring in your favorite chair from your previous home, pictures on the walls that you enjoy, records, family photos, books, or an entertainment center. Being surrounded by familiar objects helps to make a strange apartment or house a home. You and your kids will all find comfort in this way.

What's Cookin'?

In the beginning you may find yourself taking your kids out for a special treat at the closest fast food joint, partly to get through meals as quickly and easily as possible but also as a way of saying, this is our special time together. This is okay for awhile, but don't make it a way of life with your kids. Obviously, it's unhealthy; our kids are growing fat on hamburgers and French fries. But there's more to it than that. Mealtime is an important time. When your kids see you cooking for them, or you invite them to help you prepare a meal, you are sending them a solid message that you care about them in this special way. When you sit down to eat with your kids, it's a time to talk and exchange information about your day. It's an excellent way to find out what's happening with each other, and lots of data shows that eating meals together results in better family relations.

At this point in human evolution, gender roles have broken down for some of us. More men than ever are cooking, for example, and in a great many families they cook most of the family meals. But if you don't know how to cook anything more than soup, beans, and hamburgers, no problem: start there, and then expand your repertoire. If you don't already know what your kids like to eat, find out. Ask your spouse, if she is the one who did most of the shopping and meal preparation. Involve your children in the shopping as well as the cooking. But set some limits, remembering that children are prime targets for advertising, and the food that gets the biggest ad budgets is often loaded with sugar and/or preservatives. So whether you like it or not, you're going to need to look at issues like what's good (and what's not so good) for your children to eat.

RESOURCES

 If you are just starting out and want some good solid references to help you in this new venture, try *The Joy of Cooking*, by Myra Rombauer (Scribner), or *Better Homes & Gardens New Cook Book* (Better Homes & Gardens).

If you really are looking for something basic, try *The Absolute Beginner's Cookbook*, or *How Long Do I Cook a 3-Minute Egg?*, by Jackie Eddy & Eleanor Clark (Gramercy).

Is there a vegetarian in the family? Get a copy of *Laurel's Kitchen*, by Laurel Robertson, Carol Flinders, and Brian Ruppenthal (10 Speed Press).

And here's a tip if you are not into spending a lot of money on cookbooks: Check the used bookstores. Their shelves are usually well-stocked with cookbooks of all kinds. Or go to the Internet: www.epicurious.com makes it easy to search for recipes by ingredient or type of cuisine.

Excuse Me! Do I Look Like a Taxi?

Well, the answer to that question, from the vantage point of a 10-year-old who needs to get to soccer at nine on Saturday morning, across town to his friend James' house for a birthday party at one, and then back to Mom's by seven because Grandma is coming to visit, is definitely "yes!" You are running a taxi service. And apart from the hour and a half that you'll be watching soccer practice, it may be that the only time you're going to have with your kid that day is in the car as you shuttle from place to place. It's not exactly what comes to mind when you think of the phrase "spending quality time with your children," but on some days, it's all you have and it'll have to do.

You'll need to juggle your own schedule around theirs. Are you all alone in this venture? Not necessarily. You and your kids may already be part of a carpool, with parents joining together to share these responsibilities. You'll probably know if your kids are already in a carpool, and if you weren't the parent who did the driving you'll have to find out the details from your ex.

If public transportation is available and your child is old enough to handle it alone, this can be a godsend. But before you encourage this, check out the route yourself. With your child, take exactly the route the child would use and make sure that it is a trip your child can manage safely. If dependable taxi service is available in the area where you live, consider setting up an account with them to pick up and deliver your kids at certain times and on certain days. Over time, one particular taxi driver will probably be assigned to your kids. This service can be expensive, but if your work schedule conflicts with pickup times, it can be well worth it.

Another alternative, if you have scheduling conflicts, is to hire a college student or retired person to do some of the driving. You might find someone who can pick up your kids, care for them for an hour or more while you're still at work, and maybe even do a little grocery shopping for you from time to time.

Finally, most schools these days have after-school programs available. Look into what your child's school offers, for it can give you an extra hour or more to get from work to school. These programs can be excellent or poor, depending on the people who are supervising. The best of them try to balance playtime, help with homework, and socializing. Get permission from the principal to observe the program in action before you enroll your kids.

Remember You're Human

Nobody who's ever been through what we're exploring in this book ever claimed it is easy. It's not. The situation stinks, there's no doubt about it. And the most challenging part of it is trying to meet your kids' needs at a time when you are feeling anything but strong and sure, including making a new home that will work for you and your kids. It's vital that you hold steady and do your level best to manage each situation with patience and with your focus on your kids' well-being.

Put yourself in your kids' shoes. Think about how difficult it is for them as victims of a situation they had no part in creating. And as part of establishing a new home life for them, let them know that you understand how hard the transition is on them. Assure them that you're going to work through it and in just a little while things will start feeling a whole lot better for everyone—for them, for Mom, and for yourself. Tell the kids—again and again—that even though you and their mom no longer live under the same roof, you both still love them and will always be there for them. Your love for them won't stop just because you and their mom aren't getting along.

While you are setting up housekeeping and getting your separate lives organized around the kids, other parents can become powerful allies. You may find a helpful cohort in your carpool or at the playground where your kids are practicing soccer on Saturday mornings. If you don't know it already, you'll soon discover that parents are great networkers, sharing resources such as rides to the park or to school. But it doesn't stop there. If your kid is having trouble at school, ask for advice from other parents on how to handle it. You won't always get easy answers, but you'll get ideas and support. Take care to cultivate easygoing and reciprocal friendships. Be diligent about paying back favors that are extended to you, even if all you can offer at the time is a sincere thank-you, with the invitation to call on you if the person who helped you needs a hand.

As soon as you feel able, reach out to your former wife and let her know that you will do everything in your power to establish a positive collaboration with her, particularly where the kids are involved. When you have the kids for an extended stay, be sure to report back to her how they did, how they ate, and whether or not they had any difficulties that you think she should know about. Be sure to report the good things that happened, not just the problems. And never, ever imply that somehow her parenting was to blame. Create and build, always with the faith that your positive and supportive efforts will strengthen your kids and allow them to feel good about themselves.

When you have difficult moments with your kids, and they share their discomfort about what they are feeling, give them something to build on, to have faith in. Explain to them that just like a bruise or other hurt, the discomfort or pain they are now feeling will, in time, go away. Let them know that whenever they want to tell you how they are feeling, you will do your best to listen really, really well and try to make things better. Let them know that they are not alone in having divorced parents. Lots of kids in their school are going through the same thing. Nobody finds it easy, but everyone makes it through.

Taking Stock

When you are beginning your new home life and adjusting to the new world order in your family, it's an excellent time to take stock of who you are and what you want from life. Where do you want to be five years from now? Ten years? Think about what's ahead of you and make plans about what you'll do to get there.

RESOURCES

 If you want to spend some concentrated time thinking about your present and future, here are some resources for taking stock and planning ahead.

Now, Discover Your Strengths by Marcus Buckingham, Donald O. Clifton (The Free Press). Teaches readers how to live most days from a place of strength, rather than involving themselves in activities that continue to weaken them.

The 7 Habits of Highly Effective People by Stephen R. Covey (Simon & Schuster). True success encompasses a balance of personal and professional effectiveness, so this book is a manual for performing better in both arenas. His anecdotes are as frequently from family situations as from business challenges.

Think and Grow Rich by Napoleon Hill (Random House) First published in 1937 and arguably the best book on (the technology of) success. Not too comprehensive, but if you are ready to work for success, it tells you all you need to do in order to achieve or accomplish whatever you want. ●

CHAPTER THREE

Daily Life as a Single Dad

It's not just the big things that change when you get divorced—it's all the little things, too, like when you get up in the morning and what you do after work. As a single dad, of course, you don't have the luxury of simply creating the schedule that works best for you and your kids—you also have to take into account your ex-wife's scheduling needs. Working together to solve all the little logistical problems that pop up may be the first big test of your resolve to deal cooperatively with your ex, for the sake of your kids and your own sanity. It may take a while before the bigger picture falls into place and you can

A schedule defends from chaos and whim.
—ANNIE DILLARD

arrange a weekly, monthly, or annual schedule that you know will work for everyone. Right now, focus on one day at a time—getting yourself and your kids off to work, school, and extracurricular activities.

Divorcing dads frequently discover how much they and the kids have depended on Mom taking responsibility for getting everyone to the right place at the right time. Often the primary parent keeps all those schedules in his or her head, along with a list of organizations and activities the kids are involved in and the names of teachers, program supervisors, and friends to call in an emergency. Sometimes the biggest challenge is transferring that list of contacts from one spouse's mind to the other's address book.

So, what is it like to have joint custody, where you have your kids with you for more than just the classic every-other-weekend schedule? Not all fathers have this arrangement, of course. Maybe work makes it impossible for you to share joint custody. Maybe the distance between your place and the kids' mom's place makes joint custody impractical. Or perhaps you and your ex agreed that it wouldn't be good for the kids to shuffle them back and forth between your homes. Even if you don't have joint custody—or if you don't yet know what your custody or visitation rights will be—it can be helpful to consider what joint custody might look like.

A Typical Day

Here's one scenario of a fairly typical day for the divorced dad with shared custody:

- **6:15 A.M.** Alarm goes off early enough that you have time to shower, shave, dress, and get yourself ready for the day before you wake up the kids and all your attention turns to getting them ready. Somewhere in there you start the coffee, put breakfast stuff on the table, and toss some dirty laundry in the washer.

- **6:45.** You wake up the kids and begin getting them ready for school. The younger your kids are, the longer this process will take—it'll likely require some cajoling on your part, as well as the occasional intervention to help find the right color socks, help them on with a pullover, and find the sneaker that the dog decided to hide in the cat's litter box the night before.

- **7:15.** You supervise breakfast while getting lunches packed and getting books and other school materials into the kids' backpacks. While you're doing this, you are eating your own breakfast, drinking your coffee, and mentally making sure that you and the kids all have everything you need for the day.

- **7:40.** The kids are off to school. You're either driving them yourself or taking them down to the curb or the corner to be picked up by the carpool or bus.

- **8:00.** If the kids were picked up at home, you might have an opportunity to take a deep breath in your own house. Of course, while you are doing that, you're probably also cleaning up the kitchen. You then gather your stuff and you're off to work.

- **9 to 5.** You're at work. During the day, your ex calls you because the kids' medical insurance premium is overdue. You handle it between work responsibilities. At 5 you make a mad dash for the parking lot. You've got a 30-minute commute on a good day, and the babysitter who picked the kids up from school at 3:30 needs your kids out of her house by 5:40 at the latest, so that she can start dinner for her family.

- **5:40.** You've picked up the kids and are on your way home. Your son reminds you that you are out of milk and bread, so you stop at the convenience store, which means that you arrive home at just a bit past 6.

- **6:15.** You cook some hamburgers and make a quick salad, and you all sit down to eat together.

- **6:45.** With dinner over, the kids get to watch a half-hour of TV while you clear away the dinner rubble and stick some dishes in the dishwasher. It's then you remember you put some things in the washing machine before you left home that morning. You toss those things in the dryer and make a quick cruise through the kids' room, straightening up the worst of the mess before returning to the living room, shutting off the TV, and getting the kids to break out their homework. You pay some bills and review some work while they do their schoolwork, making yourself available for questions if they have any. (For older kids, you may have to allot more time for homework.) When they're done with their homework, it might be bath time for some or all of them, then storytime for the younger set before bed.

- **8:45.** The children are snug in their beds after only token protests. Ahhh, a bit of time to yourself. It's delicious but you're exhausted. By 9:30 you're sound asleep on the couch.

Sound hectic? You probably already know that this is the best-case scenario, the one in which you keep to your schedule, someone remembers that you need to stop at the store, and there are no unexpected twists or turns. Then there are the not-so-good days, the days when everything that possibly could go wrong, does.

On Less-Than-Ideal Days

One winter morning, you and the kids leave your cozy apartment to go out to the freezing-cold car and discover your battery is dead. Road service is backed up for two hours. You frantically call people on your networking list. Turns out the only person who can help is your ex. She gives you a lecture about keeping your car in better shape—the price you pay to find out that on the plus side, she's willing to pick up the kids and get them to school. You thank her when she arrives, and make it to work only an hour late.

The rest of your day may go smoothly, but you're probably drinking in the reality that organizing the daily routine involves much more than just keeping a calendar of everyone's appointments and activities. In fact, the happiest solution you can imagine right now is that the gods will look down upon you and magically provide you with a social director-psychotherapist-driver-babysitter-teacher-cook all rolled into one. As if organizing your work and social life around your kids' needs weren't enough of a challenge, you are probably going to discover that very heated and intense emotions will be entering into the picture. These emotions can include yours, your ex-wife's, the children's and anyone else who might come into your family's life. Consider the following scenario, drawn from a real-life situation.

Aaron and Marlene divorced when their two daughters were teenagers. Like so many families these days, everyone was deeply involved in outside activities. Marlene was getting her degree at a university 70 miles away; 14-year-old Shauna was taking a class in computer graphics at the community college; Lilly, 16, was a violinist in the school orchestra and had practice after school twice a week. The logistics of everyone's comings and goings had been working pretty well before the divorce, but setting up separate households presented all four family members with new challenges. They'd discussed the logistical problems before Aaron moved out, but actually meeting everyone's needs after the move was harder than anybody had anticipated.

Thanks to a friend moving out of his apartment just a few miles from the family home, Aaron found a decent place to live, with room enough for the girls to share a large bedroom with its own separate bathroom. That much went smoothly enough. City bus service ran between the two households as well as from the girls' school to Aaron's new place. They thought that might simplify some of their transportation needs.

Originally the girls were to spend three days a week with their father and four days with their mom. But within a few weeks, Aaron discovered how much the whole family had depended on Marlene to make the schedule work. In the past, Aaron had given the transportation issue his attention only when something went wrong or a change in someone's schedule necessitated that he fill in.

Despite their careful planning, the first few weeks of the separation were disastrous, putting everyone on edge. On the very first day that the girls were with Aaron, the community college student he had hired to drive Shauna home at 3:30, thus allowing Lilly to stay for orchestra practice, broke his leg during football practice. He wouldn't be able to drive for another month. Aaron had to leave work early to pick up his daughter and bring her home.

The next day Aaron let Lilly take his car to get herself and Shauna to and from school while he got a ride from a coworker. At 3, Lilly called his office to tell him the car had a flat tire and she didn't know what to do. Meanwhile, when Lilly didn't arrive to pick her up, Shauna took the city bus home, something she'd never done before. Aaron called road service for Lilly and frantically telephoned Marlene to have her check to make sure Shauna arrived safely. When he got home that night after work, he found an angry note from Marlene, saying she'd taken Shauna home with her and that she thought it was irresponsible of him to send her home alone on the bus without checking out the route first.

Although they kept trying for another week or so, transportation for the girls during the days they were at Aaron's home simply wasn't working out. He needed Marlene's help. The bottom line, he thought, was that her time was more flexible than his and she would just have to make herself available on those days when the kids were with him. He would sit down with Marlene and the girls to work things out and hopefully his ex would see the light—but he wasn't looking forward to that, and for good reason. On the day Aaron moved out, Marlene had told him, in no uncertain terms, that she would not be responsible for taxiing the girls around during the days they spent with him.

While her declaration certainly made it difficult to think about starting a negotiation, Aaron very much hoped that Marlene would be able to bend a little, set aside her anger, and let her children's needs take precedence. He fully understood that she wanted to put distance between him and her. They were, after all, separated and on their way to being divorced. But the kids had needs that they were both equally responsible for, and that fact could not be ignored.

"To be perfectly honest," Aaron told his men's group that night, "I had this naive idea that the divorce would make my life easier. Wrong! In some ways, we communicated better when we were married and fighting. We'd fight our way to some kind of arrangement that we could both live with—at least for awhile."

Others in the group agreed that divorce doesn't end the relationship; it only changes it. And changing it can be difficult on a daily basis, and confusing in relation to the big picture, in various ways. After Aaron spoke, another man said, "I started asking myself, if we were able to work these things out after the divorce, why couldn't we do it when we were married? It certainly made me have second thoughts about the whole thing."

Aaron and Marlene were just at the beginning of the learning curve of their post-divorce relationship. Married or not, they both loved their children and were determined to work together for Shauna and Lilly's best interests.

Aaron and Marlene agreed to have a preliminary telephone conversation about their children's transportation problems. But their first efforts to communicate went awry, and Aaron ended up slamming down the phone in utter frustration. The moment he did, he realized that getting mad and withdrawing would only exacerbate the problem. That much he'd learned from couples counseling two years before. After taking 20 minutes to calm himself down and give himself a pep talk, he called Marlene back and apologized. He confessed later that this took a great deal of intestinal fortitude, particularly because he felt there should have been two-way apologies, but none was forthcoming from Marlene. While not exactly in a collaborative mood, he nevertheless recognized that he would need to put aside his own feelings long enough to at least discuss the business at hand. At last Marlene agreed to meet with him and the girls in person. They set up a date for the following week.

The night before the meeting with Marlene, Aaron presented his problem to three friends from his men's group. All three had been through similar challenges in their divorces. One of the men had this to say: "I'd always prided myself in being a pretty good negotiator—but having to work things out with my ex, especially during the first year or two of our divorce, really challenged me. My butt was to the wall more than once and, I must admit, I got pretty stubborn. I believed I had to assert myself if I was ever going to get my way about anything. In the end, that proved to be a mistake. It was when we started presenting things as choices—decisions that were open for negotiation and that we needed to make together—that we finally made some headway. And as much as I hate to admit it, that was my ex-wife's idea."

Aaron got many helpful tips like this from his friends. They coached him in applying some collaborative skills, such as the 24-hour rule that you'll learn about later, that ultimately allowed both him and Marlene to keep their daughters' needs in the foreground. Both parents found they could make certain compromises without giving away their own power. The first of those compromises was to pool their funds and buy Lilly her own car, something they had discussed before their divorce. She already had a driver's license and thus could take on a good chunk of the taxiing responsibilities for herself and her sister. Once they did that, things eased up quite a bit on the transportation front. Aaron also offered to pay Marlene additional child support in exchange for the extra time and expense she would put in taking care of transportation, and she agreed to that.

The next big challenge for Aaron and Marlene was a more emotional one. This came about six months later, when Shauna made friends with other kids in Aaron's neighborhood. Dad's house, rather than Mom's, began looking like home base for Shauna. The day arrived when she announced that she wanted to go to her mother's house only on weekends, so that she could spend five days a week nearer to her friends. Marlene felt terribly threatened by Shauna's demand. In a family meeting that Shauna and Aaron initiated, Marlene was able to express how she felt. She was afraid that her own child was rejecting her. She suspected that Aaron had said something to alienate Shauna. She also felt like Shauna didn't need her anymore.

"I still love you, Mom," Shauna told her mother tearfully and completely spontaneously. "It's just that I'm nearly 15 now and I've got my own life." Marlene wept, Shauna hugged her, and in the end gave in and allowed her daughter to spend one more day per week at her dad's. As they were saying goodbye after that meeting, Marlene took Aaron aside and said, "I'm not ready for our kids to grow up. This is very hard." This family, as all families do, was changing. Moreover, they were beginning to work together to ease the adjustments that were needed. Both parents realized that along with the adjustments they were making because of the divorce, the normal changes children go through as they grow up, including their growing independence, require adjustments from the parents. The adjustments that parents must make during children's adolescence, in particular, can be a challenge even in families where everyone is living under one roof.

Aaron started out wanting to protect himself from showing any vulnerability in his negotiations with his ex-wife—but as a result of that meeting about living arrangements, he saw that he didn't need to be quite so guarded. Over time, Aaron and Marlene's relationship evolved until they were able to cooperate pretty well about things that involved their daughters.

Their story is fairly typical, especially in one respect: After setting up separate households, one or both parents may have some rude awakenings around scheduling even something as straightforward as transportation.

Managing the Details

When you were married, who handled most of the logistics of the family's activities—you or your wife? If you are the one who kept the schedules straight, put yourself in your ex-wife's shoes as you are making the transition. Recognize that true collaboration begins with making all of the information about the logistics available to her. If you have a list of other parents or friends on whom you've depended to get the kids around to after-school activities, make a copy of this list for the children's mom. If some of the names require explanation, such as how that person can be helpful or whom you'd only call in a pinch, be sure to write it down. If you find yourself resisting, put your kids in the foreground of your consciousness and remind yourself that you are doing this to make their life easier.

On the other hand, if your ex-wife has been handling most or all of that, it's very possible that you'll be finding yourself taking on responsibility for things that you completely took for granted in the past. Don't overlook what may seem like minor items, such as getting the kids to share the chores, monitoring their behavior at mealtime, making certain they do their homework, or arranging carpools to get them from place to place. Be sure you tell your ex you want all the information you'll need to take on your share of the responsibility for the logistics of the kids' lives. What you need to know will depend on a multitude of factors, including how old your kids are, how much time they spend with you, what activities they are involved in, where their friends live, any special health problems they may have, what you want the mealtime schedule to be, and your work schedule.

A FEW PARENTAL TASKS—AND THE INFO YOU'LL NEED TO MAKE THEM HAPPEN

Here are of some of the things you should expect to do as a custodial parent with lots of time with your kids. (If you're the primary parent now, consider sharing it with your ex-spouse.) It's not exhaustive, but it should provide some food for thought, and you can expand it to include the specific responsibilities of your family.

- arranging for baby sitters or after-school care
- organizing after-school activities such as sports, classes, or clubs: getting your kids enrolled, scheduling transportation, and purchasing special clothes or equipment
- arranging for visits with friends
- scheduling haircuts, checkups, and shots
- picking up presents for birthday parties and getting the kids there
- dealing with special health problems: scheduling doctor visits, and making certain that teachers and caregivers know how to administer medication and handle any emergencies
- shopping for groceries, clothes for the kids, and other necessities
- scheduling consistent mealtimes
- planning for illness, school holidays, and summer vacation: what happens when the kids aren't in school and you have to work?
- meeting with teachers, other parents, coaches
- arranging transportation between parents' homes

In order to make all of this work, both parents will need certain important phone numbers:

- Doctor and dentist
- Insurance companies
- Human resources at whichever employer provides insurance
- School administrators and teachers
- Kids' friends, with parents' names and numbers

- Classes and lessons
- Babysitters
- Carpool drivers
- Relatives who can help out

And finally, make sure that each of you has all the information about any medications your kids take, and any allergies or other medical issues they have.

If at all possible, avoid reinventing the wheel. Try to maintain your relationships with other parents and continue the arrangements you had before the divorce, if the geography of your living situation allows it.

THE FAMILY DOG (AND OTHER CRITTERS)

If animals are a part of your family, think carefully about how you will accommodate them in the new family order. Will the landlord at your new place allow animals? Will you need to find a new home for this valued member of your family? If that's the case, how will the kids handle it? Consider the fact that animals require time and caring, just as your children do. As any dog owner knows, dogs develop strong emotional attachments to the families in which they live. The family becomes the dog's pack, responsible for meeting its needs. When families break up, companion animals may become insecure and fearful. And in fact, they've got good reason to worry. Sometimes family pets are put up for adoption or even euthanized.

While the fate of animal companions may not be uppermost in your mind at the time of your divorce, do your best to consider their rights and their welfare. While you may not have been the one to bring them into your family in the first place, someone in your family wanted them and, like it or not, that saddles you with the responsibility of dealing with their fate. And don't forget that animals can be important sources of comfort for kids whose lives are disrupted by the divorce—losing a pet on top of losing the existing family structure can be pretty tough.

Caring for Your Kids

Joint custody arrangements give children the opportunity to spend significant amounts of time with both parents, generally a positive thing for kids during divorce. (Chapter 6 discusses joint custody in detail.) True joint custody also requires a high level of collaboration between the parents on the day-to-day care of their kids. If the children are splitting their time between your house and their mom's, it's especially important to keep communication channels open and clear between you, your ex, and your kids.

Some of the issues you'll need to work out are obvious, while others are more subtle. Here are some everyday issues you'll need to deal with.

CALENDARING. You and your ex (and the kids, if they're teenagers) will need to keep joint calendars. This includes not only where the kids stay each day and night, but also their schedule of activities. Keeping these calendars current is essential, requiring a high degree of cooperation from everyone. Collaborative skills will be particularly important here.

CLOTHING AND RELATED ITEMS. Do the kids keep extra wardrobes at your house, or do they transport everything back and forth? Be sure to get a second set of toiletries and grooming items for your kids, and make sure you have your kids with you when you shop for them--especially if they are in the pre-teen or teenaged years. Children (like adults) can be very choosy about this stuff.

COOKING AND EATING. Make sure you are clear about what's okay for your kids to eat and not eat. You may want to indulge them with their favorite snacks, especially in the initial stages of the new living arrangements, but if you don't maintain some controls over eating habits from the start, you may be contributing to a food problem in the future. If you are not familiar with the kids' diets—and many fathers are not—be sure to sit down and get advice on feeding them.

SHOPPING FOR FOOD. If you have the kids with you on a regular, scheduled basis, you'll probably find yourself grocery shopping with them. If this is a new experience for you, be sure to take the time to figure out a good routine. Kids generally like to go to the supermarket with mom or dad, but you'll quickly learn that there are a million products that your kids know about and simply must have, and you may tire of holding the line. Usually they've learned about these magical, essential (and usually expensive and unhealthy) items on TV. Depending on how old your kids are, there may be lots of excitement, begging for this or that, and crying when you tell them no. Set clear limits from the start and stick to them.

You'll eventually work out your own routine, in your own style, but for the first few trips to the store with your kids, focus on teaching them good behavior—no nagging, no crying, no running in the aisles (even if they don't usually behave like this, they'll probably be testing your resolve). Limit the first shopping trips to picking up no more than a dozen items. In that way, you can make the focus of the trip a learning experience—for you and for the kids!

ALLOWANCE. It's a good idea for older kids—seven and up—to have an allowance. Allowing them to handle their own money can be a good way to teach them financial responsibility. Coordinate this with your ex rather than giving two separate allowances, one from you and one from their mother.

HOLIDAYS. During the big nationally hyped holidays, such as Thanksgiving and Christmas, when there is tremendous pressure for families to come together, anxieties tend to be high even under the best of circumstances. Handling holidays smoothly after a divorce will require considerable collaborative skill. Try to schedule your children's time with you well in advance—in fact, months in advance. This will avoid conflicts in planning. And you'll have to take into account, especially as the children get older, that they need to have a say in where they go. They may want to spend time with friends, not just family. As with every other decision you'll make about dealing with your kids, it's really important to listen carefully to the child's needs and desires. You won't always be able to satisfy them, but you should try your best to really pay attention to what the others want, and look within yourself to see whether you can make it happen. Don't say no just because you're attached to a particular notion of how families spend the holidays— consider what really will work best for who your children actually are, and don't be afraid to give a little. Remember that this collaboration thing doesn't stop with you and your ex; it must include the kids.

There's much more about holidays and birthdays in Chapter 9.

CHORES. A friend told me the story of a large family in the town where he grew up that drove around in one of those big GMC Travelalls, the 1950s precursor of the Hummer. On the side of the vehicle was a carefully painted sign that said: "Confusion Incorporated." The story went that the father of this family, with seven kids, was a corporate attorney. He had literally structured the family around the corporate model, with each person assigned a specific position (Dad was the CEO, Mom the CFO, and so on) and responsibilities. My friend didn't know how well the organization worked, but one could speculate that the name plastered on the side of their vehicle probably reflected the reality. Whatever the underlying truth about Confusion, Inc. might be, the idea of assigning roles and responsibilities to the kids is a good one. Even younger children can "help Dad" with simple tasks such as picking up toys after playtime or putting yesterday's newspaper into the recycling bin. If you take care to assign tasks that are age-appropriate, the kids' help really will ease your load and also give the child a sense of making a valued contribution.

BATHING. Depending on your previous arrangements, you may or may not have been involved in getting the kids bathed and in bed at night. If you're not familiar with the bathing routine, check with the kids' mom and get the lowdown. For younger kids, close supervision is mandatory and will require a good chunk of time—usually just before bedtime, but sometimes earlier in the evening. Older kids can take care of their own hygiene, but sometimes they need reminding—do you know the last time your teenager had a shower?

LAUNDRY. Okay, in college you did your own laundry, unlike your roommate who mailed his home every week for his mother to do. But are you really aware of the mountains of dirty laundry one active child can generate in just a few days? A top priority when you're looking for your first post-divorce home should be laundry facilities on the premises, if not right inside your abode. If you depend on a trip to the laundromat, it's a trip you'll have to schedule. What do you do with the kids while the Maytag is grinding away? And when do you make time in your busy day for that?

So you know how to turn on the washing machine and you get the difference between normal and fluff dry. Next you can learn about fabric softener, environmentally correct detergents, bleach, and spot removers. And of course, you surely know about washing the whites separately!

HEALTH ISSUES. Who takes the kids to the doctor and dentist? And where do you go when your four-year-old falls down on her tricycle and cuts her lip? Many dads these days are familiar with these caretaking duties, but if these are unknown destinations for you, get all the necessary information from your ex. Emergencies are a part of growing up. Most of them are minor, if a bit bloody, but be prepared by knowing where to get help when you need it. Knowing the route to an urgent care center or hospital can save you a lot of anxiety on that rare (with luck) occasion when you and your child might need it. As for the routine appointments, they are, in most cases, only a couple of times a year. Still, you and your ex will need to work out who takes the kids for their annual checkups or their teeth cleanings.

Baby Sitters and After-School Care

Obviously, if the kids get out of school at three and you get out of work at six, you're going to need some help. Your two basic choices are an after-school program of some kind, or a dependable and mature caregiver with whom you are confident your children will be safe and well-nurtured.

With two working parents more the rule than the exception in today's world, after-school care is available in many communities, through the schools and various private programs. Many of these programs offer a variety of playtime and educational activities, so they can be excellent options for your kids.

The after-school programs at public schools are generally not free, though many offer sliding fee schedules that can help out if you're in need. Even with the best babysitter or after school care, you'll have to schedule in enough time for picking your kids up, maybe chatting with the teacher or other parents, and possibly stopping at the store on the way home—not to mention time-consuming extras you didn't anticipate.

TIP

DON'T BE LATE! If you do put your kids in an after-school program, pick them up on time. There's usually a significant extra charge if you do not—like $25 for the first time you're more than 10 minutes late, $50 the next, and after that you're outta there for good.

Homework, TV, Games, & Leisure

One thing this world does not lack is electronic diversions for children. Between the Internet, digital game devices, and television, a child can be involved in passive or robotic stimulus-response activities for days on end. Electronic toys are engaging and even hypnotic, and they are generally devoid of reasoning, aesthetics, and the emotions of human interaction. Some content is sensational and two-dimensional at best and downright destructive at worst. Child development experts recommend that time with all such activities should be limited and screened by parents. For the parent, this isn't easy. After a long day at work and a list of things that still must be done at home, having the kids mesmerized in front of the TV can provide a welcome and much-deserved breather.

While your children are in your care, however, you need to pay attention to how they are spending their time. How many hours are they spending in front of a TV or computer screen? What are they watching, and what are the commercials they're being subjected to in the process? What are they doing on the computer? The Internet provides all kinds of risks—kids can find sites that are entirely inappropriate, and chat rooms can lead to dangerous real-life encounters. What video games and CDs do they have? Watch enough of them that you can determine the kinds of values and human relationships these entertainments are modeling for your kids.

Look also at the time your children spend with their homework and reading—and with you reading to them. Time spent reading books together, snuggled up together on the couch or in bed, is the kind of time that creates a special bond between parent and child. Not only do the children have the experience of reading, but the closeness of this time together is precious to them. Don't try to "teach" during this time. Choose books that are fun and pleasurable to read, ones that will activate the children's imagination.

And what about homework? Even younger children get homework these days. If you have any questions about the kinds and amounts of homework your children are being assigned, check with their teachers. Often parents ask, "What if I don't have any background in what my child is learning?" Never fear. In most cases, you don't have to know. Tell your child outright that you don't know and then ask them to teach you. This reversal of roles is one of the best teaching devices around. In explaining things to you, your child is forced to think about the topic. Helping you understand helps children understand and will even deepen their appreciation for their own knowledge and boost their self-esteem.

And then there are times when you've just got to dig in and find out more about what your child is studying. If you need help, the child's teacher is your best resource. Usually that means making an after-school appointment with the teacher, but you may be able to get the information you need by email or over the phone.

I asked several teachers I know what advice they would give fathers about how to handle homework responsibilities. All said the same things:

- Set a regular time for homework.
- Turn the television off.
- Suspend any activities going on in the house that might be distracting to the student.
- Create an atmosphere conducive to study. If you have letters to write or anything that you may have brought home to do for your own homework, do it during the time your child is studying. Your involvement with your own homework provides an excellent model.

All of this takes time and patience, as you probably already know. The payoff is not just good grades, but children with greater respect for their own knowledge, a sense that self-discipline can bring rewards, and high self-esteem.

"Right Speech" and Staying Focused on the Future

Part of establishing a daily routine is figuring out how to communicate with and about your ex, and that means making sure you watch what you say even when circumstances are adverse. When you check in with friends and acquaintances, you may find that some have turned against you—possibly because they were more your ex-wife's friends than yours in the first place, or possibly because your ex has engaged in trashing you a bit. After all, most people in the midst of a marital breakup vent to friends, and under these trying circumstances it's pretty difficult to keep perspective—so it's unlikely that your mutual friends and acquaintances are getting the whole story.

Having spoken with hundreds of divorcing fathers over the years, I count on one hand those who have gone through divorces without a period of trashing the partners they were separating from—or being trashed by them. It may go on for several years after the divorce. Sure, it's small, petty, and mean-spirited. But try to keep it in perspective as one of the ways we have of distancing ourselves from a person with whom we have shared an important part of our lives—and whom, in many cases, we still love. That doesn't mean it's okay to do it, but remember that collaborative divorce requires holding a broad perspective of understanding and compassion, not just for our ex but also for ourselves.

The best thing you can do is to acknowledge and accept that some of the people who once helped you and your ex-wife may not feel like extending the same favors they did in the past. Do your best to let go of any emotional charge you have around them, particularly if holding that charge gets in the way of allowing post-divorce collaborations to evolve.

True Stories: Rude Awakenings

One young man, Jesse, remarked, "My ex and I had this great friend, Belinda, who I'd always thought was pretty neutral about our divorce. She was always trying to reassure me this was the case. So when she didn't return my phone calls for several weeks I went over to her house to find out what was up. I never even got a foot in the door! She called me a liar and a coward--and those were her milder accusations. I was really pissed. There was no room for discussion, she just plain dumped on me and wasn't going to even try to hear my side of it."

The Buddhists teach that "right speech" is essential for a satisfying life. Right speech means telling the truth, refraining from unjust criticism of others, using language constructively rather than harshly, and refraining from gossip. Following these principles can go a long way toward creating and maintaining a collaborative divorce. But because avoiding the truth, criticizing others, using harsh language, and gossiping are all ways that we vent our pain when a relationship breaks up, it's far easier said than done. Neither you nor your ex will always measure up to those goals. But try to keep these tenets in mind as best you can. The more successful your efforts, the more likely you'll create a collaborative relationship with your ex.

CHAPTER FOUR

The Noncustodial Dance

Being a noncustodial parent has unique challenges, not the least of which is the emotional toll of being separated from your kids. Even if you have chosen to be the noncustodial parent and you know that the decision you and your ex-wife made is the right one for your kids, it isn't easy.

I know; I was a noncustodial dad. I certainly missed being a part of my children's daily lives after the divorce. I had a particularly difficult time around holidays, birthdays, and events like first dates and my younger son's first time playing soccer goalie and first confrontations with a homeless panhandler in San Francisco. When my ex and I lived quite near to each other right after the divorce, I was active in the kids' after-school activities and day-to-day lives. Later, she moved about three hours away and I started to drift away emotionally as well. It wasn't intentional, that's for sure, but I sensed the distance growing. I needed to encourage myself to go the extra mile and stay connected with my children.

> *It doesn't matter who my father was; it matters who I remember he was.*
>
> —ANNE SEXTON

When I saw that too much time was elapsing between phone calls and visits, I began making more conscious and deliberate efforts to stay in touch. Each week, I'd mark days on the calendar to be sure to call. When birthdays and holidays were coming up, I made a note to plan special get-togethers with my kids. I looked forward to my time with the kids and I enjoyed thinking about upcoming events when I could buy a nice gift, or planning times when I could simply phone with something to share about my own life.

I remember looking for any excuse to send a little gift—a stuffed toy when my daughter was little, or a poster or a CD that I thought one of the kids would like. While these gifts didn't take the place of a father's love and presence, they were important reminders of the love we shared. All my children have told me that they looked forward to my regular phone calls and visits. They never doubted I was still very much a part of their lives, and they knew that I never stopped caring about them and taking pride in being their dad.

There were certainly times when I felt depressed, missing my children and wishing I could spend more time with them. I had to make an effort to pull myself together and show up for them—and also to stay in close touch with my ex-wife, so that we could continue parenting together effectively. That part is definitely not easy, especially in the early stages when you're still angry and disappointed, but you must do it. Stay in touch however you can and gracefully let go of any illusions you still have about being able to control minor issues. Just be sure you're on deck to handle the major ones when they come up—and they will.

Dealing with the Changes

It takes time to adjust to being the noncustodial parent, particularly if you're accustomed to spending time with your kids every day. For a long time after the separation, your life can feel very empty, though in some ways also simpler. Not much to do when you get home at night! But without the kids in your daily life, you can get a bit lonely or even depressed. As one man put it, "For months I felt shipwrecked. Every night after work, I returned to my empty apartment and felt like I'd just landed on a desert island."

It's tempting to look for ways to fill the void. Some men do it by finding a new lover or looking for a new job or taking up a new sport or hobby. It can feel like it would be easier to not see your kids at all, to move to another state so that the wounds of separation won't be reopened every week or two by a visit from the kids. A new lover, a new job, a new city, or finding new friends and new activities will all keep you from thinking too much about your life and can bring some instant relief, it's true. But you will start thinking about your kids again. You can't escape the reality that they are out there and they want you to be in their lives.

What works during the early stages of discovering yourself as a noncustodial dad? If you want to get this thing working for you and the kids as quickly as possible, get some help. This could be a friend who has made the leap across the gap and is content with the arrangement he's developed with his kids and ex-wife. It could be a pastoral counselor who is able to help you process some of your feelings and help you get more focused and clear. Or it could be a psychotherapist. If you haven't done any inner work exploring who you are and what you're about, now's the time. Swallow your pride and hurt feelings, do some work on your anger and whatever other issues you might have, and stay put. Do not leave town. The kids need their dad, and you need the kids.

The bottom line is that as difficult as this time is, try to relax, take a deep breath or two, and use it as an opportunity for personal growth.

True Stories: A Tale of Two Cities

When Jane and Rob divorced, Rob was in the middle of changing jobs. In fact, the last straw, as Jane saw it, was that Rob unilaterally decided to take a new job—1,000 miles away—even though she had said she would never consider moving. Moving would mean pulling the kids, Marsh and Tricia, out of school and after-school activities they really loved and away from friends they'd grown up with. Rob, however, was just as adamant about the career move, which was a major advancement and offered a 35% increase in pay. It was his dream job and there was no way he'd turn it down.

Jane and Rob had discussed divorcing before the job offer was even on the table. Both had attorneys and they had worked hard to figure out what they would do if they separated, so when they got down to drafting their final separation agreements, they were able to come to a relatively amicable settlement. They mutually agreed that if Rob took the job, Jane would keep custody of the children and Rob would provide financial support, making it possible for her to be a full-time, stay-at-home mom. Rob considered Jane a great mom and wanted this stability for his kids. Being highly motivated in his career, he knew that if he had primary custody he would have to hire a live-in nanny. So with the children's best interests in mind, he chose to be the noncustodial parent. He would, however, organize his work life so that he could spend short blocks of quality time with his children throughout the year.

Rob had no intention of giving up any of his rights as Marsh and Tricia's dad, even though he had chosen to be the noncustodial parent. Rob and Jane agreed that Rob would have an equal say about the children's education, any medical issues that might arise, social freedoms and responsibilities such as dating when they were older, and vacation planning. This last issue was particularly important to both parents because it would be during vacations that Rob would be scheduling his time with the kids and Jane would have time to herself.

While the changes in this family's life went relatively smoothly, Rob soon found that he missed his kids far more than he'd ever imagined. He wasn't there the day Marsh had a bad tumble on his bike, requiring several stitches to his forehead. Nor was he there for the Spring pageant in which Tricia played a forest nymph. There were also the evenings when Jane called to get Rob's support with a behavioral problem from one of the kids. Even this way of being included in the parenting process reminded him that he was no longer participating in their day-to-day life.

Even before the divorce, Rob's time at home had been limited. Like many fathers who are actively building their professions, businesses, or careers, he had often left the office at eight or nine in the evening, arriving home after the children were already in bed. He missed a lot of what went on in the house during the day. He always heard about victories and conflicts after the fact. From 1,000 miles away, he felt more emotionally distant than ever, and found himself feeling nostalgic about experiences he'd been just as happy to avoid at one point in his life. In some ways, he now participated in the challenges of parenting more than he ever had, though it involved long phone conversations with both his ex and his kids, helping them in whatever way he could to navigate the rougher seas of their lives.

There was still a great deal of tension between Rob and Jane, but they had learned to be civil with each other. They were at least able to solve the problems they needed to solve without too much conflagration. After two years, Rob began to regret moving such a long distance away. One year later, Rob found a job less then two hours away from the kids. Although the job meant a pay cut, he jumped at the opportunity to be closer to what he called home.

Some Things Don't Change

Never lose sight of the fact that your children are still your family, though you are no longer living in the same house and may even be living miles and miles away.

Many single fathers I know worry that without their daily guidance the kids can easily go astray, either because the home situation is not ideal or because they might fall in with a bad crowd at school or in the streets. Fathers also worry that their kids will lose interest in them or stop loving them, or will think that Dad doesn't love them anymore. However, parenting experts and psychologists tell us that it is not the amount of time you spend with your kids that counts so much as the quality of time you spend with them. Even if you spend only weekends with your children, or perhaps only vacation periods, you are still a very powerful and important influence in their lives.

Similarly, the mother of your children is still the mother of your children, and that will never change either. As such, she too is a member of your extended family. If this is too much to take in right now, relax. It simply means that if you want to have things go as well as possible from here on out, you can't deny that your ex is going to be in your life—at least until your kids are independent and able to have a relationship directly with you, without her facilitation.

Which brings us to another question: Will you ever get over the tension you feel when you're around your ex or when you're having to negotiate visitations or other issues with her? Maybe, and maybe not. All of these issues of the heart tend to get exaggerated when you're the noncustodial parent, in part because you have more time to think about what's happened to your family and to stew over the past (and sometimes, the present and the future as well). But that doesn't mean that you can't treat each other with respect.

Accept what your relationship is today, with no backward looks at what was or what you hoped it would be. This acceptance of what is true for today will help you take the high road throughout the divorce process and beyond.

The trick is to acknowledge what is and make your peace with it. This is not for your ex's comfort or peace of mind but for yours and your children's. In most cases, it is possible to turn a difficult situation into a much better one. No matter how you might be feeling right now, trust me when I say that you now have a chance to create a better relationship with your kids, your former wife, and with yourself. There's a lot of potential for powerful growth and healing during this transition. This is a time to summon up your courage and begin to turn disadvantages into advantages.

Staying Connected

If you're a dad who has been pretty involved in your kids' daily lives and activities, it's a weird feeling to have "visits" from the children you used to live with. Your kids will definitely be feeling that, too. Your job is to acknowledge those feelings in you and your kids, and resist the temptation to allow the strangeness of it all to loosen your connection to your kids. Here are some tips about making the transition—and as you'll see, it doesn't involve taking the kids to Disneyland every weekend, but requires you to continue being present for them in a daily way.

Your children need to feel that they are in your thoughts even when they're not with you physically. There are as many ways to do this as there are families. One man in a divorced father group told me how he connected with his daughter during time they spent apart. His daughter loved to read, a passion she shared with her father, who was an English teacher. The two of them passed books back and forth, sharing ideas from the books they read and discussing how the books taught them something about their own lives. They wrote to each other nearly every night. It was a wonderful way for these two to stay in touch, for the literary conversations often spilled over into personal issues.

You can also help your kids know that they are present in your thoughts by having evidence of their place in your life throughout your new home. For example, display photos of them throughout your place. If you have artwork they've done, put it on your walls. If they have given you gifts over the years, make sure those gifts are in evidence when they come to visit. One dad I know tells the story of how his daughter gave him an apron to wear when he was cooking and doing kitchen chores. Across the front were big red letters that said, "My Dad is cookin'!" He hated that apron. It stayed in a kitchen drawer whenever his daughter wasn't there, but when she visited, out it came. They even went through a little ritual of her tying it on for him each time she came to visit. This simple ritual sent his daughter a message that she had a permanent place in his life, one that didn't go away when she went home to Mom.

I had an architect friend who had divorced when his son, their only child, was four years old. I was always fascinated by how my friend held his little boy in his lap while he was working at his drawing board. He always set the boy up with a piece of his own drawing paper, pinned near Dad's drawings. The child contentedly drew pictures on his paper while Dad worked on his. This, to me, was the essence of quality time between a father and his young son. It was no surprise, years later, when the son became a book illustrator and cartoonist. That time together at the drawing board was not only a time of bonding for father and son but apparently got the son in touch with a natural talent that would later be the basis of his career.

How you create quality time together with your children is up to you. You'll find the secret is in choosing something you can do together that you're genuinely interested in, that your kids are interested in, and that you have fun doing together. If the activity requires a certain level of physical or mental development, always be patient and accept your children's efforts without critique. Do it for the pleasure of sharing this time and allowing your children to develop skills at their own pace. Remember, the quality of the relationship counts far more than a finished artifact, a home run, or a ball thrown directly from point A to point B.

It's easy, as a noncustodial dad, to worry that your children no longer get enough guidance from you. But don't try to cram it all in during your weekend visits—your kids don't need long lectures from you or heavy-handed guidance when you're together. Just as when you lived together full-time, what you do will make a greater impression than what you say.

And the kids certainly don't need to hear you trashing their mom—even if you feel she deserves it. What they need is your attention focused on them in the most loving, caring way you can do it. That's best expressed by being present with them and listening to them, letting them know that their feelings, their thoughts, and their accomplishments and challenges are important to you.

Different Voices, Different Homes

One of the reasons you and your kids' mom divorced was probably that you had slightly—or maybe dramatically—different ways of looking at the world. While it's true that people divorce for a wide variety or reasons, differences in their fundamental views of how things should be done is often at the heart of their conflicts. This makes the chances quite good that after divorce, your kids will be going back and forth between two households that may be worlds apart. There may be different rules and expectations, different aesthetics, different physical comforts, and even a different level of material goodies available.

Should you work for consistency between your two households? The consensus from both men and women I've talked with is that the better solution lies in recognizing and accepting diversity of opinion and lifestyles. You don't have to agree with how your ex-wife does things, but things will go much better if you can respect her choices. If you do, you'll also be a great model for your kids—the parents I talked to said it was important for their kids because it taught them to be comfortable with differences. For these families, conflicts still arose from time to time, but the experience of learning to live in two different households was generally beneficial. Of course, if there are special problems, where the children's well-being is at stake, then you will have to take action. The best approach is usually to seek the help of a family therapist who can advise you not only of your rights and responsibilities but of what you can do to ensure the children's safety right now.

I was one of the lucky ones. My ex-wife and I nearly always agreed upon the important stuff and would back each other up on such things as dealing with failing grades, teenagers staying out too late or being defiant, getting tattoos (no!), as well as what consequences would be imposed for acting out. We did not want run each other's households—not any more. And our disagreements mostly came from not listening to what the other was saying. Once we stopped and listened carefully, we were always able to come to agreement about how to parent together.

Try not to take a defensive posture about differences between the two households—even if you feel that your ex-wife is trying to "one-up" you. Let the child know that you are aware of the differences and they don't bother you. If you model a belief that each way of being deserves respect, your kids will pick that up.

True Stories: Rich Dad, Not-So-Rich Dad

Gene tells how his ex-wife remarried a man who had a good deal more money than Gene did. Kimball, the new husband, had a huge house in an upscale neighborhood, fancy cars, and even a yacht. Gene, who was a college teacher, had a far more modest lifestyle. When Gene's son Sam was about 12 he started putting his father down, telling him how his stepfather was a lot richer than him. Gene was hurt, of course, and his first reaction was anger.

After calming down a bit, he told his son, "You are really lucky to have Kimball as a stepfather. It's great to be able to afford stuff like he has. But I chose to have a different kind of life. I love teaching and working with students, and I wouldn't trade that for anything. You're right, though, I don't have the kind of money Kimball has. College professors just don't make a lot." After this talk, Sam never mentioned his stepfather's wealth again.

Establishing Your House Rules

Letting go of any efforts to impose your lifestyle, values, and desires on your former spouse doesn't mean you can't have your way in your home; in fact, you definitely should. Create your own schedule for family dinner and your own rules about homework, television, and social or free time. This is a natural way for you to build a trusting and whole relationship with your kids. They'll know where you stand, and that is always a good thing.

Of course, kids being kids, you're likely to get arguments such as, "That's not the way Mom does it." Or, "Jerry [the stepfather] lets me use his computer anytime I want." Your answer, always, is to stick with who you are: "That's fine, son. When you're at Mom's house, I want you to mind her and do things the way she likes you to. But you're here now and this is the way we do things here." Present your position with no judgment and no comparisons that might indicate that you think your way is better. Ultimately, the best lesson you can teach your children is that there are different ways to do things, and while you don't insist that yours is the only way, it's your way and it's how you expect them to do things with you.

In establishing rules for your new home, be true to what's important and comfortable for you. Keep rules simple and logical and you'll get much less resistance from your kids about following them. For example, you might have a rule, with children old enough to handle it, that they carry their own dirty dishes to the sink after a meal. The logic is that it makes your job easier so that you can spend more time with the kids, helping them with homework, playing, or watching a TV program together. Also, everyone lives in the house, and it takes everyone to make it a good place to be.

It is important to establish these rules early so that your children associate them with being at Dad's house. It's a when-in-Rome-do-as-the-Romans-do kind of thing. And it's a great idea to ask for input from the kids so that they can feel invested in this process, and understand the reasons behind the rules. You're probably familiar with the rules that your children have to follow at their mom's, so whenever you can reasonably do so, transplant those rules to your house—as long as they coincide with your way of living and beliefs. You may be surprised at how some house rules are pretty universal, even when deeper differences exist between you and your ex. Most of them, after all, are aimed at keeping the place functioning effectively, instilling values, or protecting your kids' safety—think of things like curfews, manners, and respect for others' privacy. Aesthetic concerns like the cleanliness of common areas is more of a personal issue, and you and your ex may differ on that without causing too much confusion or stress. In addition, you might have religious or spiritual rules that you want followed in your home, such as offering a blessing before meals or saying evening or sabbath prayers.

Do not criticize when your children tell you how things are done at Mom's. For example, if your kids argue that Mom doesn't make them clear the table, don't come back with, "Yeah? Well, your mother lets you kids run her life, too, but you're not getting away with that here!" Instead say, "Okay. That's fine. Do it Mom's way when you're at Mom's house. But here, we all help."

Especially because your time with your kids is so limited, you'll want the time to be pleasant and fun; and you don't want to spend all your time policing a bunch of rules. But making your expectations and standards clear to your children will actually help build rapport with them and cut down on whining and conflict. These boundaries are healthy for them, and establishing them is part of your job as a parent. Children want to know what you expect of them, and the sooner you make your expectations and standards clear to them, the better things will be. Even though the kids spend less time with you than with their mother, they still need to know what you find acceptable and what you need from them.

If you or the kids' mother are working on a behavioral change at home, you'll want the other's support. This could be any number of things, from toilet training to manners at the dinner table to doing homework to practicing a musical instrument. If the kids' mom tells you she'd like you to follow through on that program when they are with you, do everything in your power to support her efforts. Maybe you think she overemphasizes table manners or healthy eating habits. Or maybe you're still angry and hurt and the last thing you want to do is cooperate with her. If that's the case, unless you're practicing for sainthood this isn't going to be easy. But step back for a moment and remind yourself that by collaborating and helping your kids' mother, you are ultimately helping your children.

BEING THE BABYSITTER

One of the things that can be tough for noncustodial dads is feeling like just the babysitter. As divorced dad Dominic put it, "I know damn well she calls me to take the kids every time Mike, her lover, comes to town. It's like a dagger in my back when I think about it—me taking the kids so she can spend the night with her boyfriend." Still, Dominic usually agrees, no questions asked, because it gives him more time with the kids. By focusing on them and his own relationship with them, it takes some of the sting out, and he invariably ends up having a good time.

You may feel taken advantage of when your ex asks you to spend an extra evening babysitting or calls you on short notice to take the kids to a lesson or appointment after school—it's a common point of friction for divorced spouses. The bottom line is that you'll need to be flexible with the custody and visitation schedule. This doesn't mean that you should become a doormat. But you'll all do better if you can cut each other some slack now and then.

There's lots more about parenting collaboratively in Chapters 7, 9, and 11.

Getting Flexible at Work

Some employers offer flextime or telecommuting, allowing employees to work at home some of the time or arrange their hours to work longer hours over fewer days. As long as you produce what is needed, your employer may be willing to honor such an arrangement. If you work at home and don't have meetings, you may have the whole day to get a specific amount of work done, but whether you finish at five p.m. or at midnight might make little or no difference.

For noncustodial parents, flexing your work hours can be a way to get in a little more time with your kids. If your work time is flexible, you may be able to:

- Volunteer for after-school events.
- Volunteer to help out in the classroom.
- Taxi the kids to wherever they need to go that day.
- Become an assistant coach for an after-school athletic program.
- Give extra help with homework.
- Do some shopping with the kids for clothes or other things they need.

You might also just make a few extra points with your ex if you make extra space for the kids in your week. Look upon your efforts as feeding the collaborative spirit, as well as benefiting you and your kids by giving you more time together. Don't forget that there will be times when you want or need cooperation from your ex—for example, when your car is in the shop and you want her to drop the kids off at your house. But it doesn't have to be quid pro quo—maybe you just want her to know that you're not such a bad guy after all, and that you recognize how important it is to work together for the benefit of the kids—and to make each other's lives as easy and comfortable as possible, despite the fact that you're no longer married.

Show Up When You Say You Will

When you are first getting used to the noncustodial parent role, you might not have the routine down yet. For example, you might not know how long it takes to get from work to pick up the kids on a Friday night when traffic is heavy. While that's understandable, try to work these things out ahead of time so that you can show up on time. Being even 20 minutes late can cause significant anxiety for your kids and your ex. (At the very least, give a call on the cell phone to say you're on your way.)

I can't stress strongly enough that you must make this an indelible rule in your own mind: Show up when you said you will. If you say you'll be there at 7 p.m., be there at 7 p.m. Whatever you do, never, ever call at 6:35 to say you can't make it. The kids count on you to be there, and they will be hurt if you're not. And they will take their cues about being reliable from you. Like it or not, you are a very important role model in their life: you're the dad.

It's stressful enough for your kids to have parents living in two different houses, and to have to shuttle back and forth and spend time with their parents separately. Don't add to their burden by being a dad who makes lots of promises but can't be counted on to deliver. Trust me on this one. I have promised things I failed to deliver. At the time I might have tried to tell myself that there were extenuating circumstances that caused my failure to show up—and it might have even been true. Even so, afterwards I felt like crap, and later on the kids let me know how disappointed they were.

Of course, if you have a real emergency and are late to pick the kids up once, don't beat yourself up over it. Just don't make a habit of it. Everyone understands an occasional cancellation, but recurring ones means that you are really not showing up for your kids.

Presence, Not Presents

I suppose there exists in the dark and mysterious recesses of every divorced father's mind some element of guilt. My experience is that even when everyone agrees that the divorce was exactly the right thing to do, we still feel regrets for our kids and wish that we'd had the power to make their lives a little easier. Your feelings are natural, but don't let them lead to actions that can send the wrong signal to the kids. That includes trying to make up for what we regret with material things—in short, overcompensating. A friend related the following story about the child of a woman he was dating. Felix had been dating Sheri for about three months and had noticed that her daughter, Shauna, who was four at the time, seemed starved for male attention. She asked Felix each time he came to visit if he was going to be her daddy now. Each time, it was very embarrassing for him, but he made it quite clear that he was Mommy's friend and Shauna's friend, too.

One day, after Shauna had been put to bed, Felix asked Sheri what was up with Shauna. Did her father take an active interest in her life? Sheri shook her head. "He lives only ten miles away but he thinks all he has to do is send her a toy now and then and everything will be okay." She beckoned to him and stood before a closed door. When she opened it, he saw stuffed toys, mostly all kinds of teddy bears, piled three feet high and wall-to-wall. There was hardly enough room to enter. "Except for his support check," Sheri said, "this is the extent of what Shauna knows of her Daddy. He sends her stuffed bears."

While extreme, this example isn't totally off the wall. The take-home message is to realize that what your kids want from you is not stuffed toys or video games and CDs but your presence and caring in their lives. Deliver this and you won't slip into being a guilty-feeling dad who doesn't show up when he needs to and tries to compensate with material presents. You'll know and value yourself and be open to giving of yourself and enjoying your time with your kids. While you might be feeling guilty or remorseful for blowing it on rare occasions—it is still important to not shower the kids with gifts, money, or too much freedom. You are their parent, which means it's your responsibility to set boundaries. Don't spoil them—that's what they have grandparents for. And believe me, it won't work in the long run.

Your kids need a father. Toys, vacations, and parties every weekend may be okay, but not if you are giving those things because you're feeling too guilty to give of yourself. Your kids need you to be present on a regular basis, as a caring, accountable, and responsible father. This is the best gift you can ever give your kids, and it is one that they will cherish all their lives. It is also a gift that you are giving to yourself. ●

CHAPTER FIVE

Ex-Communications:
10 Ways to Make Talking to Your Ex Easier

You and your wife probably divorced because you couldn't work out the conflicts you encountered in your life together. But now that you've separated, you're not off the hook on working stuff out. The fact is, as long as you have kids together, you and your ex are still going to have a relationship, and some of the same issues you had when you were together are going to carry over. There's no doubt

that this is a different relationship than you had before, but it's a relationship nevertheless. Now you are faced with coordinating responsibilities involving the kids—everything from signing them up for after-school activities to saving for their education. All this coordination requires good communication—without it, you can't have a collaborative divorce.

This chapter is intended to be short and easy-to-follow, with no frills— just ten tried-and-true ground rules for good communication during a collaborative divorce. These rules reflect a boundary that we should all respect: that each of us is a human being with a unique set of strengths and weaknesses. We deserve each other's respect—even though we might have very different ways of looking at the world.

Following these guidelines, alone or together with your ex-spouse, will make life easier for everyone involved. If you are the only one implementing them, have patience. In time, these practices will rub off on your ex—as well as your kids, by the way—as everyone begins to reap the benefits of the collaborative approach.

I'm not promising that all of this will be easy. In fact, it, will probably be quite hard in the beginning. Have patience, give it time, and things will improve.

WHERE ARE YOU ON THE CIVILITY SCALE?

In the heat of addressing emotional issues, logic and reason often take a backseat—or never even get aboard. It's easy to recognize when another person's emotions are overriding good sense, and less easy to recognize when it's happening to you. When you're facing a stressful situation with your ex, it's a good idea to assume that your emotions are driving you, rather than assuming that you are the only one being logical or reasonable. Let go of any illusions you might have that you can manage others' emotions, and instead put your efforts into managing your own. Your ability to do this will probably be determined by where you and your ex fall on the communication continuum:

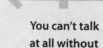

| You can't talk at all without really losing it | You and your ex can have limited civil discussions, but it doesn't take much to go into a major meltdown | You regularly have civil discussions with your ex |

Most of us would like to always be able to have a civil discussion, but in many cases we simply can't manage it. That's where the guidelines below become most helpful. Be honest with yourself about where you are on the continuum at the moment. Then build skills, using this book and whatever other resources you might find useful, to help you move from wherever you are now to a point where you and your ex can work more collaboratively.

10 RULES FOR COMMUNICATION: IN BRIEF

1. Be nice

2. Spare the kids

3. Get help from third parties

4. Take 24

5. Create clear boundaries

6. Don't try to change her

7. Find ways to agree

8. Listen to your ex without defending yourself

9. Let your ex have her way without giving up yours

10. Ask for what you want

1. Be Nice

Sounds simple, doesn't it? But a little politeness can go a long way. This is the time to try hard to be nice—meaning simply be polite to the greatest extent possible. Try not to be rude, call names, or speak in anger. Especially in the beginning, often a look, an offhand remark, or a gesture will send you toward an attacking or defensive mode. Resist it! Sometimes, something as simple as putting your hand on your own stomach or chest will ground you and calm you down to where you can relax a bit and concentrate on having a civil conversation. If you're not able to do that, invoke the 24-hour rule (discussed below) and take some time to calm down before having the conversation—politely.

2. Spare the Kids

You don't ever want your kids to take sides or be in the middle of the hassles between you and your ex-wife. While you are rebuilding your relationship, you're going to try to be nice, as noted above. But it's crucial that you are at least civil to each other when the children are around. This might take some effort, but keep in mind how terribly hard it is for kids to be in the middle. If you take their interests to heart, your self-esteem will rise knowing you are sparing the kids from the most stressful parts of your interactions with your ex.

And no matter how angry and hurt you are after communicating with your ex, don't ever release your frustration on the kids. Even if you feel like your ex is making things crazy for you, and even if you believe she is bad-mouthing you to the kids, do not involve them in your conflicts or concerns. Remember: they need both parents, and one parent should not recruit the kids against the other parent. Take it from me—it will only come back and cause everyone pain, especially the kids. You do not want your children to be held hostage in an uncivil war.

3. Get Help

If your relationship with your ex-spouse seems to be all about shouting, slamming doors, and hanging up phones, it might be time for some third-party help from a therapist, spiritual advisor, or mediator. A third party can help you get past the emotions and establish new ground rules for collaborating. You can hire a family therapist to help—it is cheaper than a lawyer, and introducing a lawyer at this point can make things turn nasty pretty fast. The therapist can help with communication between you and your ex-spouse. In some instances, it will also reduce the time your lawyers spend haggling over issues you should be able to talk about and resolve. If you don't want to see a therapist, but you and your spouse share a spiritual or religious tradition, you could ask someone you both trust to help you with your communication. You could also seek out a mediator, who could also help with decisions that need to be made in the course of your divorce. Whatever you choose, you will save yourselves, as well as your friends and family, a lot of grief if you get some intervention instead of continuing down the road of conflict and strife.

4. Take 24

In the early stages of my divorce, I had real trouble dealing with immediate challenges. When I was pressed to make important on-the-spot decisions while feeling angry, hurt, or vulnerable, I'd agree to things just to end the hassle. Then I wound up resenting the decision. I could have used 24 hours to think things over clearly.

There is a period of negotiation in any divorce, when both parties are working out what they need and what they can live with. The 24-hour rule is an easy way to avoid making impulsive mistakes during stressful talks with your ex. It's simple: Any time you are faced with a decision, insist on taking 24 hours to think about it. When you know you have this cushion, it's much easier to handle emotions that are triggered by whatever proposition requires a decision. Having this cushion assures you that you'll have time to think things out, and maybe even do a little research or get some advice from a friend.

5. Create Clear Boundaries

Boundaries are enormously important during your divorce. If you don't draw a line regarding what type of treatment you will accept now, how will your ex-spouse ever know how you expect to be treated? If it's not okay for her to call ten times a day, tell her it's not. If it's not okay for her to call you insulting names, call her on it and let her know that in no uncertain terms. The fact that you are divorcing demonstrates that you and your ex no longer have a good sense of what makes each other tick—though you may have an unerring sense of what ticks each other off. It is now time for you to express how you want to be treated and accept nothing less then that. What do you have to lose? After all, you are already divorcing. The flip side of this is that you will need to respect boundaries that she sets, as well, and look honestly at your own behavior when she states those boundaries.

6. Don't Try to Change Her

When you were married, no doubt there were things you wanted to change about your wife. Now that the marriage is over, those same things are probably still bugging you as you try to work out the details of post-divorce life. Remember, you could not change her then—and you can't now. Accept and even honor her right to be who she is. You can't control her behavior, but you can always control yours. If you refrain from trying to change your ex, after a bit of time, she might feel the shift and respond positively to it. You don't need to announce your new approach—just quit struggling to get her to be different. The absence of that power struggle should go a long way toward creating a more balanced relationship between you.

7. Find Ways to Agree

Solving minor hassles is very good practice for solving major hassles that are really stressful. If you have a habit of cooperating, you can fall back on it and make an agreement that in turn helps build a more permanent foundation of cooperation in raising your kids.

The best way to get started is to try to find things to agree on wherever you can, and then remind each other about those, rather then focusing on the things that don't work. The bottom line is that both of you love the kids and want the best for them—try to work with your ex-spouse to build on that.

8. Listen to Your Ex-Spouse without Defending Yourself

How to listen to the concerns and often, the complaints of a sometimes angry ex-spouse is a constant theme for many divorcing couples. At times it can be very difficult to actually listen to what our ex is saying because we too are angry, as well as absorbed in our own defenses, desires, and attachments. We may also simply disagree with what our ex is saying. Whether we are "right" or justified in our position is not the issue. The goal is clear and easy communications that will better support the kids' well-being. Start by being a good listener, which can be harder than it sounds. The most effective way to listen is to refrain from defending your position. If you can manage it, it's good to ask some questions about your ex's concerns, so that you can be sure you really understand them.

OPEN-HEARTED LISTENING

Open-hearted listening is what's called for in the collaborative process. The key lies in the simple act of allowing what others say to exist, without trying to change it. Breakdowns in relationships often occur not because of what is said, but because of what one is unwilling to hear and acknowledge as true for another. You earn the right to speak through giving the gift you most want to receive—sincere, open-hearted listening even if you:

- have hurt each other before
- believe you hate each other
- don't trust each other, and
- have never done it before.

Not defending yourself does not mean giving in to something that you don't agree with. It does mean not reacting to the hot buttons that will naturally be pushed when your ex-wife is complaining about you. Take a breath. Be calm. At this point, when you're feeling on edge, it is best to invoke the 24-hour rule. Just say that you need 24 hours to consider anything and you don't want to react out of emotion before you answer. This will give both of you a cooling-off period.

This advice will help get you through the difficult conversations without too much stress. To go even further would be to actually look at what your ex is saying, and consider whether any of it might be true. For example, she may be complaining that you are consistently late picking up the kids. Your first reaction may be to defend yourself by listing all the things that are stressful about your job and that keep you from being on time and reminding her that you need the job in order to pay child and spousal support. Another option would be to take in what she is saying, and brainstorm ways that you could get out of the office on time on the days that you are meeting the kids.

Admittedly, it's especially difficult if the concerns your ex is raising are ones that you've been over a million times—or ones that you feel are just flat-out wrong or unfair. But try to be open to feedback about your own behavior; you may find yourself learning things that will help you to grow into the father that you want to be.

9. Let Your Ex Have Her Way While Not Giving Up Yours

Life is full of trade-offs and compromises, and divorce is no exception. But if you act graciously in relation to the small problems, in most cases you will have some bargaining power when it comes to issues that really mean something to you. I am not recommending that you give up things that are important to you. That will only make you resentful and angry. However, I am suggesting that you don't sweat the small stuff.

10. Ask for What You Want

Rather than being defensive, holding out, or forcing your ex-spouse to guess what you really want, practice clearly asking for what you want. If you want more time with the kids, want to take your favorite easy chair from the house, or need her to be more patient when you are trying to formulate your thoughts, be calm and just say so. Don't assume she knows what you want. You might not always get it, but you can ask, and you might be surprised at the results.

This is another good place to bring in the 24-hour rule. If you make a request of your ex, ask her to think about it for 24 hours before deciding. If she's resistant to what you want, gently point out the times when you have given in to her wishes—if you've followed my advice, you will have in fact done that at times. This give and take is what collaboration is all about.

11. Bonus Advice:
Ground Rules for Face-to-Face Meetings

You might wish that, at least for a while, you could avoid your ex-wife completely. But it's seldom that simple. If you have young children, you'll probably need to hand them directly to their mom after you've had them at your house. And you may need to meet to discuss practical aspects of your divorce and co-parenting arrangements. These meetings can be explosive, especially in the early days or when you may not be getting along very well. Here are some ideas about how to make the process as painless and productive as possible.

- Have a list or agenda to discuss and stick to it. Don't throw in other issues or change the subject.

- Start all discussions with appreciation—even if you can only find one thing to appreciate about your ex, remember to say it.

- Take one issue at a time, confirming each agreement before moving on to the next.

- Discuss how you will review or refine a decision you've made together, setting times when you might revisit the issue or have a progress report.

- Agree on a process for refining a decision if it isn't working as well as you'd both like.

As you are considering these points, don't overlook what may seem like obvious, practical considerations, such as when to have meetings, where to have them, and what to do with the kids in the interim. Consider meeting in a neutral place. It can be painful to go back to the home you've left, with all the emotional associations you have with the place. As one divorcing father put it, "Jill and I sat in the living room with the kids playing in their rooms upstairs and I couldn't concentrate on our meeting at all. I thought it would be okay, but it wasn't and I finally just had to excuse myself and leave. After that, I made arrangements to meet at a friend's office after business hours and that was much better."

There are plenty of issues to decide when you are divorcing, from the very simplest—like who will close the joint checking accounts—to the most complex about what will be best for your kids. You are not going to handle everything at one sitting. It will be an ongoing process, so become accustomed to working together for the sake of the kids. How you communicate now will be the basis of your new relationship with your ex, and your relationship now will set the stage for your new family culture. ●

CHAPTER SIX

Settling Up: Legal and Custody Issues

So far, this book has been mainly about the practical and emotional work of divorcing—dealing with yourself, your kids, and your ex as you learn about the changing landscape of your family. But of course divorce is also a legal process—and going through it will test your determination to put anger aside and work toward collaboration.

> *Divorce is only less painful than the need for divorce.*
>
> —JANE O'REILLY

The day you consult an attorney or file your divorce papers is the day that a whole different relationship begins to evolve with your soon-to-be ex-wife. Difficult feelings and arguments the two of you have been struggling with privately are now being discussed with a stranger who knows little more than your name and what you can pay. And getting lawyers involved can, if you're not careful, cause tensions to escalate almost immediately, until the very center of your relationship has become a skirmish over money, control, and visitation rights. As Nicholas, recently joining the corps of divorced fathers, bitterly told his men's group:

"I was so unprepared for this step. I hired an attorney I'd picked out of the phone book, he filed papers, and suddenly I felt like I'd been caught up in a tornado. What I wish somebody had told me was how adversarial things can get, that if you thought you were at war before, you've got a lot of surprises ahead of you. You don't know what war is, or can be, depending on how the whole thing is working out."

Nicholas happened to get an attorney who had a particularly adversarial approach, and there certainly is no shortage of them. However, in recent years many divorce attorneys have taken a different approach, especially where children are involved. If you try, you can find a lawyer who will support, rather than undermine, your desire to have a collaborative divorce process. (See "How to Choose an Attorney," below.)

But before you even bring in lawyers, try working out as many agreements as you can between you. This will save both of you time and money. The more you hassle, the more it costs and the more likely it is that you will end up in court. And as my own lawyer friends are quick to point out, the legal system is no place to work out any conflict as deep as the emotions of marital conflict. At the point that you and your ex see that things are heading for the courts, try backing off and seeking out an experienced mediator or therapist. In most cases, it will make your life much easier, and you (and your kids) will have fewer wounds to heal after it's all done. Who knows, you may even heal some festering wounds along the way.

At this transition point, there is a single principle I wish that every divorcing father would adopt as an inviolable practice: Do everything you can to avoid hurting the kids. And never forget that if you hurt their mom you're probably going to be hurting them. Not easy advice to follow. When we are under fire, it's hardwired into our system to fight back, preferably with the big guns. I've been through it and I know. Nevertheless, it's immensely important that you avoid saying or doing anything to inflict pain on your ex, even if you are treated in a cruel or totally unsympathetic way, and even if you are convinced that what your ex is doing is wrong. It's up to you to do no harm—or at least no further harm. This is the essence of the collaborative approach, and this stage of the relationship is where it is most difficult to practice.

There's a wonderful quote by the author of *The Process of Intuition* (Theosophical Pub House), Virginia Burden Tower. She points out that a relationship of cooperation rather than combat begins with "a thorough conviction that nobody can get there unless everybody gets there." In other words, you won't ever be done—really done—with the separation and divorce process if you and your spouse don't work through the process together.

This chapter will give you some grounding in the legal issues that you'll need to deal with during your divorce, and offer advice on getting through what can be a painful legal process without losing your bank account or your dignity—and without inflicting damage on your kids.

The High Cost of Conflict

When we're angry and hurt, and our financial coffers are under siege, let's face it, most of us are inclined to declare war. And it's not just a guy thing. Under fire, women can easily be as warring as men; they just have somewhat different tactics and weapons.

But if you maintain a warring attitude while trying to settle the legal aspect of your divorce, it's going to cost you—and cost you big. So before you put on your armor and drag your weapons into the courtroom, let's review the rules of collaboration and compassionate engagement. From the outset, you'll be seeking an outcome based on the principle that nobody gets there unless everybody gets there. Is this always going to be possible—for everyone to end up in agreement in the end? No. But you need to do everything you can to hold that intention.

If your ex is incredibly angry with you, or you with her, or if either of you gets a contentious lawyer, get ready to cash in your life savings. Contentious divorces wreak havoc on thousands of families every year. Couples spend enormous sums of money arguing over property or, even more painfully, over custody of their children. All of this money goes to lawyers, accountants, custody evaluators, and other professionals, instead of toward the kids' college educations or other benefits for them. Often, the outcome of the contest is very similar to whatever compromise proposal both parties rejected in favor of the drawn-out battle.

Sometimes, even when you don't want to have a contested divorce, circumstances get away from you.

True Stories: One Wrong Move

Gordon, a patent attorney, didn't anticipate the trouble it would cause when he hired his friend Jarred to handle his divorce. Jarred had earned a reputation for being a "street fighter" divorce lawyer, and had built his whole business around his ability to handle very contentious, high-stakes divorces. But that wasn't why Gordon sought his help. "I hired him because he was the only divorce lawyer I personally knew," Gordon explained. "Besides, he is really a nice guy outside of court, and I like him a lot. I thought because my wife Dez knew him and they had always gotten along fine, he'd be an asset. I didn't even think about his reputation."

When Dez, Gordon's ex, got a phone call from Jarred telling her that he was going to handle the divorce, she flipped. "How could you do this to us?" she raged at Gordon over the phone. "We agreed to keep the air clear and not hurt the kids. Now you hire the most contentious attorney in town! Why are you doing this to us?"

"I immediately realized my error," Gordon explained. "But nothing I could say or promise would make things right with Dez." He quickly hired a mediator, had his friend Jarred write Dez a letter withdrawing from the case, and hoped for the best. In the meantime, Dez had hired her own mad-dog attorney and everything got crazy. Gordon told his men's group that the damage he'd done by not thinking ahead created an atmosphere of tension that didn't calm down for nearly three years. Arguably, Dez overreacted—certainly she could have calmed down when Gordon did everything in his power to fix his mistake. But the stakes are high in the early stages of divorce, when feelings are strong and reactions quick.

Gordon's mistake and his wife's reaction to it at least doubled the legal costs of their divorce. Gordon ended up getting an attorney who worked hard to calm the churning waters, but he still ended up with extraordinary legal fees that might better have gone into his son's college fund. But the worst damage of all, he felt, was how the fallout affected his young son, who spent two years hearing what a bad guy his daddy was.

By far your best strategy is to avoid creating a contentious and hostile situation as you work out your divorce settlement. A badly handled divorce can become a never-ending source of distrust, despair, and anger. In particular, the legal phase of divorce is a time to tread lightly if at all possible. If you're not by nature an easygoing person, try to do your best imitation of one. You can go back to being high-strung after you've protected yourself, your kids, and your bank account from the consequences of reacting quickly and defensively.

I'm not saying to raise the white flag and surrender to an unfair settlement. That would likely make you more resentful and angry. But I am saying, chill out and calmly take control. If you get backed into a situation where a vigorous legal battle is absolutely necessary, be well prepared; just recognize that there's little to gain and a great deal to lose if you get mean. Remember the people who are going to be hurt include not only you and your ex, but also your children. You have at least some choice in this matter; the kids don't.

The Basics of the Legal Divorce

You are dealing with two kinds of divorce: the emotional one that requires you to restructure the intimate relationships among you, your kids, and your ex, and the legal one that requires you to understand how the divorce court system works and how the law can affect your case.

The best-case scenario is an uncontested divorce in which you and your ex agree on how you want to divide your property and share parenting of your kids. In that case, you'll probably just hire one lawyer to write up an agreement and get your paperwork filed. Most people go through a longer process of negotiating and decision-making before they come to agreement on everything. And some people never do agree, but must leave it to the judge to decide.

There are three major issues in a divorce: custody of children, support (for either the kids or your ex-spouse), and division of your assets and debts. I'll deal briefly with spousal support and property at the end of this section, but the primary focus is on custody and support of your kids.

SEE A LAWYER

 SEE A LAWYER FOR SPECIFICS. The most commonly used legal terms and custody and property arrangements are discussed below, but laws and common practices vary from state to state and even community to community. For exact information specific to where you live, you'll need to consult a lawyer or other expert near you.

SEPARATION AND DIVORCE

You may already be separated from your ex, either informally (you are simply living separately with no intention to live together again) or legally (you have court papers that say you're separated). Most people separate informally before filing papers to initiate a divorce. It's not too common to get a legal separation, but some people do it if they have financial or personal reasons for staying legally married but want to make sure their property is separated completely. When you meet with your lawyer for the first time, you can discuss whether a legal separation makes sense for you or whether—more likely—you should go forward with a divorce.

Custody

Your primary concern must be to develop a coparenting plan that is the best for the children. This is big stuff, and now is the time to embrace the collaborative process with all your energy.

Legal Custody

Legal custody means a parent has legal authority to care for and make decisions concerning the children's health, education, and welfare. Legal custody is either "joint" or "sole." Unless there is a compelling reason to keep one parent from involvement in decision-making, most courts grant joint legal custody even if one parent spends much more time with the children than the other. It means that both parents share equally in decisions that affect the kids even though one parent might only see them occasionally. Generally, courts give sole legal custody to just one parent only if the other parent is completely irresponsible and unfit to participate in decision making, if the parents' relationship is so poor that they won't be able to make decisions together, or if one parent is out of the picture.

Physical Custody

Physical custody refers to living with the children and seeing to it that their day-to-day physical needs are taken care of—feeding them, making sure they are clothed, and getting them to school on time. If you have the children with you only on weekends, on those days you have physical custody; on the other days of the week your ex has physical custody. Physical custody can be shared—called joint physical custody—even if you don't share it exactly equally. In some cases, however, the parent with a greater share of time has what's called sole physical custody, while the other parent has "visitation rights." The difference depends more on state laws and the customs of local courts than on the percentages of time.

Split Custody: Separating Siblings

In most families, siblings stay together after a divorce, often giving each other crucial stability and support—but sometimes, it's appropriate to make different custody arrangements for different siblings. For example, if one parent intends to move to another city where there's a great school system that would benefit a younger child, but the older sibling is in her last year of high school, is involved in lots of activities, and wants to stay, the parents might decide to have her live with the parent who's remaining in the original city and send the other sibling with the parent who's moving.

True Stories: Separated Siblings

Morris and his wife divorced when their children were 15 and 17. He said, "For various reasons, we decided that split custody would be best for our particular situation. My son Ross came to live with me, and my daughter Tara went with her mom. It worked out well because neither of us could afford more than a two-bedroom place, rents being what they were, and this way both kids got their own rooms. That's important for teenagers. I think if Ross and Tara had been really close, we might have worked something else out. But they had quite separate lives by then, and weren't that connected with each other. Of course, we still made sure they got together for special occasions like birthdays and Chanukah."

Keeping Custody Decisions In Your Own Hands

The issue of custody can bring up a lot of concerns for divorcing dads. For example, some fathers are afraid that if they give full custody to their ex-wife, the children will become estranged from them. Fathers with very young children may worry that they don't have the skills to care for them. Or they may simply worry that they don't have the time to deal with the day-to-day activities of the children's lives.

Decisions around the issue of custody are deeply personal and you'll need to think about what's best for you, your ex, and your kids. But one thing that's clearly best for your kids is a custody arrangement that you work out with your ex, rather than one that a judge orders.

My advice is to put your very best effort and all of your collaborative skills into working out a parenting plan with your ex. There are lots of resources that can help you with that—some of them are listed below in the section called "Do-It-Yourself Divorce," and some are included in the appendix of resources at the end of the book. Use them, and all the negotiation methods discussed below, to try to come to an agreement.

If you try your best and you and your spouse still can't agree about custody, you'll take this very personal issue in front of a judge. The judge will consider a number of factors—but a very important one is your record with the kids. Have you been a caring, accountable, and responsible parent? You will need to be able to show how you have taken (and continue to take) care of the kids and that you contribute to their well-being both financially and emotionally.

If you want an equal time-share, then you should try to establish that type of schedule from day one of your separation, even if the final details haven't been worked out. (But don't try for something that will traumatize your kids by changing what's normal for them too drastically.) If you see the kids only on occasional weekends, don't be surprised if the judge maintains the status quo and you wind up with a limited visitation arrangement. Of course, if you can show that there was a reason that you didn't press for more time during the interim period, the judge may feel differently.

TIP

If you do make an arrangement for visitation that's intended to be temporary, put it in writing. There may be reasons for the kids to spend more time with your ex while you're waiting for your court hearing, and perhaps you've reached an agreement on that. If so, write down the agreement—saying you both agree that it isn't intended to be the permanent time-sharing schedule, and that giving up some time with the kids now doesn't mean you don't want to have them for more time later.

True Stories: Things Can Change

Conrad's ex-wife, Judy, had suffered from depression much of her adult life, and when Conrad filed for divorce she became despondent. At first she clung to their daughter, Penny, saying she needed the security of at least knowing that her child would be with her. Wanting to do what was best for everyone, Conrad went along with this and did not immediately press for joint custody. In fact, at his ex-wife's request, he visited Penny only once a week. The arrangement did not go well. Judy's episodes of depression became increasingly debilitating. She sometimes overlooked Penny's well-being, failing to get her off to school in the morning and occasionally neglecting her own and the child's nutrition. Penny, who was six, was also developing signs of depression, perhaps mimicking her mother's behavior. Everyone, even Judy's own parents, became concerned.

During this time, Conrad was renting the other half of the duplex where his parents lived, and had built-in babysitters. He began to believe that Penny would be better off in his custody until Judy got back on her feet and was in better condition to care for Penny. Finally, Conrad managed to get the court order changed so that he had full custody of Penny.

Judy gave up her apartment and went to live with her parents in a nearby town. With the support of friends and family members, Judy faced the facts of her depression. She found herself a good psychotherapist and within a few months was well on her way to recovery. She returned to the city where her daughter and Conrad lived, got a good job, and rented an apartment in a good neighborhood. Today she and Conrad share custody of Penny and enjoy a genuinely collaborative relationship.

Child Support

You are responsible for the care and welfare of your children, and that means their financial support. It's best if you and your wife negotiate a fair amount for you to pay, but if you don't, the court will do it for you.

How Courts Set Support Payments

Most states set out guidelines for judges to follow when setting child support, so you can usually get some idea of what might be ordered in your case. There are websites (listed below) that will help you calculate support based on your income, your wife's income, and the amount of time you each spend with your kids.

These formulas may not always seem fair. But they were designed to guard the well-being of children, and so far, no one has come up with a more satisfactory way of establishing child support payments. Don't blame your ex for the size of the payments—remember, she didn't write the support guidelines. It's just the way our society has determined that the pie gets sliced.

Also know that these are only guidelines, and the judge can depart from them if you give a good reason. If you really think the guideline support amount isn't right in your situation—for example, if you are responsible for caring for an aging parent with lots of medical needs or have other extraordinary expenses—you can ask the judge to reduce the amount you must pay.

RESOURCES

 LOOK INTO THE BALLPARK. For free child support calculators , check out www.findlaw.com, www.familylawsoftware.com, or www.divorcehq.com.

True Stories: Don't Be a Jerk Over Money

Coming to a financial settlement when you're wounded and angry is most likely going to put you out there on the edge between reason and sanity. As Irving, from one of the men's groups confessed, "If I were a bull I'd have gone on a rampage. It made me crazy sitting there in court and hearing what was coming down. I just heard a big sucking sound and knew my financial future was getting flushed out to sea. Sure, I saw red. And I wanted revenge at that moment. But my sister had been coaching me for several weeks, reminding me that I might have to accept that I was going to be the sacrificial lamb in all this. She reminded me that I really do love my kids and want the best for them. And once upon a time I loved Lori, too, or those kids wouldn't have ever come into this world.

My sister kept telling me, 'Don't forget Lori is the mother of your
children, Irv. Be cool! Be patient. Give it space.' I'm glad I took her advice.
It took a while, but Lori and I are okay with each other now; not friends
exactly, but not enemies either."

If You Can't Make the Payments

Once the judge has made a decision, you need to face reality, pay your fair
share, and move on to create your new life. If you can't handle the payments
on your current income, you'll need to figure out a way to make up the
shortfall, perhaps by finding a higher-paying job or taking a second job.
If you cannot make a support payment, don't wait until the last minute to
contact your ex and let her know what's up. Give her plenty of notice—she is,
after all, counting on the money. If you're in an adversarial relationship with
her, you might need to notify your attorney, who can relay this info to her
lawyer, but at least you'll be on record for attempting to handle the crisis in a
responsible manner. Do the best you can by paying as much as you are able,
and then communicate clearly what you can and cannot do. If indeed you
have the money and you're just being a jerk and withholding it, get over it. I'll
make no bones about it; that's the worst kind of deadbeat dad.

If it looks like you're going to have a continuing problem making
payments, you'll need to either work it out with your ex-wife or ask the court
to reduce your payments because of your changed circumstances. After all,
married or not, people run into financial problems.

True Stories: Changing Circumstances

Adolpho was a freelance journalist who got a divorce at a time when he was riding high, with a syndicated column and lots of speaking engagements that paid excellent money. His divorce settlement and support payments took a big bite from his total income, but he was making six figures at the time and there was enough to go around. Four years later, he lost his syndication and his income dropped precipitously. For two years he lived on credit, had to sell his house, and got down to where he had only enough money to pay his basic expenses and the interest on his loans.

With Adolpho's daughter Jeda in college, his ex-wife was going nuts trying to meet expenses. One day, Adolpho called his daughter and invited her over to his apartment for dinner, explaining that he didn't have money to take her out to a restaurant. After dinner, he laid out the problem for her. He simply couldn't pay a cent for her support anymore. He was already paying her mother only half of the support he'd been ordered to pay by the court. Jeda would have to figure out what she was going to do without his support check, which was going directly to her at this time.

Jeda wept, then got angry, and then stormed out, slamming the door behind her. For the next two days, Adolpho sweated bullets, worried that Jeda was never going to talk to him again. Then, late one night, the phone rang. His daughter tearfully apologized for being so irrational and asked him to forgive her "temper tantrum." She explained that she had talked it over with her mother and two of her best friends. Her friends pointed out that both of them had part-time jobs and they were sure it wouldn't kill her to get one too. The night she called, she had just signed up for 12 hours a week of work at the college, and she was cutting two classes from her schedule.

Jeda worked and went to school part time for three semesters. After that, Adolpho was able to get back on his feet and help his daughter out a little more. By then, Jeda had grown to love her part-time job as a research assistant for one of the professors, so she kept working until she finished school even though she no longer needed to do so. She ended up with a greater sense of autonomy and solid evidence that she could take care of herself. No deadbeats here!

Be prepared to make full disclosure. If you are asking your ex or your kids to understand that you can't support them in the way the court said you must, be sure you show them the money. Be completely open about your income, your expenses, and where your money is going. If they are able to see that you truly aren't able to pay, they're more likely to be willing to understand and try to help out.

Even if your family is understanding about your inability to make your support payments, asking the court to reduce your support obligation is a good idea. As long as a support order stays in place, you are legally required to make those payments. If you don't, you are building up an "arrearage"—a debt that you owe for unpaid support. If your ex later decides she doesn't feel so understanding, she could come after you for the arrearage.

Whatever you do, don't be a deadbeat dad—one who doesn't pay support and doesn't show up for the kids. Financial problems can be debilitating, no doubt about it. And when things get too tough, and emotional pressures build up, sometimes it can feel like there's no alternative but to flake out, flee the scene, and abandon your commitments, including your kids. No matter what happens, I urge you not to do that. Your kids need you, not just your support payments.

Dividing the Pie:
Spousal Support and Property Division

Before going into any negotiation, it's important that you and your ex have a good understanding of all of your family's assets and liabilities. Whoever is helping you to make decisions about your divorce settlement will need all of the relevant information about your financial situation. You need to be aware of and have current information about all of the following:

- your income and your spouse's income from all sources
- all of your bank and investment accounts
- your current mortgage and equity line balances
- the value of your automobiles
- the value of your home furnishings and other personal property
- all of your outstanding debts, and
- other assets—don't forget things like season tickets for sporting or cultural events, 401(k) plans, and insurance policies.

Then there's the issue of what you will need to live on after the divorce, and how you and your ex will support two households. When you got married, your financial picture probably improved. As our friend Nicholas reflected, "Under one roof, two can live almost as cheaply as one...or so all your friends assure you when you're first talking about tying the knot. And it's true. Right after getting married, you shared responsibilities and that made for less stress in your life, more time to kick back, and for a while, until you learned you were going to be a father, you had two pretty decent incomes. Hey, a totally win-win situation! It worked pretty well even after my daughter was born because her mom was able to do work at home that brought in enough to cover our mortgage. It all worked okay until...well, in my case, until I started pushing to take two years off from work to do my post-grad work at the same time that our family was starting to outgrow our modest house and needed a larger and more reliable car."

Maybe you still have his-and-her incomes. But as you set up separate households, the financial burdens will definitely change. You will be looking at a neutral outcome at best, and most likely at the following additional expenses:

- rent and utilities for a second household
- new furniture and other household goods to replace what you're leaving behind
- a second car if you don't already have two
- transportation costs for the kids
- alimony
- child support
- legal fees, and
- child care.

You'll work with your mediator or therapist to figure out the best way to support both of your households. This may involve you paying support to your ex, or vice versa—the exchange of money commonly known as alimony or spousal support. Guidelines for awarding spousal support aren't as clear cut as those for child support. The first factor a court will consider is the length of your marriage—the longer the marriage, the more likely the court will award spousal support. The court will also take into account whether either spouse gave up a career to stay home and take care of the kids, or supported the other spouse through school or professional training. Especially if the stay-at-home spouse has been out of the workforce for a while, a court is likely to award support to help with retraining and reentry into the working world.

Another task facing you is to divide up your assets and debts. Everything that you own and everything that you owe will need to be divided between you, either by each of you keeping things of equal value (for example, you keep the newer car and she keeps the older one and the plasma tv), or by dividing things equally (for example, distributing half the cash in your bank accounts to each of you). For many people, their house is the major asset of the marriage. You'll need to decide whether one of you will stay in the house and buy the other out, you'll sell the house, or one of you will stay there while you continue to co-own it together for a while—something that some families do when their kids are young.

Retirement plans are another major asset that couples share. You'll need an actuary to evaluate the value of your retirement plans. You can buy your spouse out of her share in your retirement (or trade for other assets), or you can arrange for a court order requiring that her share of the pension be paid to her at the same time that it is paid to you. You'll need a lawyer to help you prepare the special court order, called a Qualified Domestic Relations Orders (QDRO), to have the pension split later.

These are just a few of the things you'll have to divide—and I haven't even mentioned your debts yet! You can probably see why having some help in working through these issues is a good idea, whether it's a therapist, a mediator, or lawyers in a collaborative process (see "The Collaborative Divorce," below). Of course, just as with custody, if you can't agree on how you will divide your property, a judge will do it for you—and you'll pay a high price for the privilege.

Do-It-Yourself Divorce

Thousands of couples each year handle their own divorces—in some states, in fact, more people go to divorce court without lawyers than with them. If your case is simple, neither of you is contesting the divorce, and you have been able to work out agreements about your property, debts, and parenting, then do-it-yourself divorce can be a good option. It'll save both of you the expense of an attorney. You can get the help you need from books and/or software designed to help you through the process. Your local family court may also have helpful materials that explain the court's rules and procedures.

How do you know whether a do-it-yourself divorce will work for you? If you answer yes to all of these questions, you may be good candidates for a self-help divorce:

- Are you able to sit down and make decisions that both of you feel are fair?

- Are you in agreement about how to divide your assets—and do you have the information that you need to do it? (Sometimes you'll need help understanding the information—for example, if you have retirement plans, you may need to get some help from an actuary before completing your divorce.)
- Do both of you have a steady source of income?
- Do both of you agree to the divorce?
- Do you have the time and skills to handle the necessary paperwork? (Check some do-it-yourself websites or books to get the lay of the land.)

DIVORCE WITHOUT COURT

There's no such thing, really, as divorce without court. Even if you and your ex work everything out yourselves, you'll have to ask a court to approve the terms of your divorce settlement. This may involve nothing more than filing some paperwork, but you will need to make sure that you follow through with everything that's required, or you won't end up legally divorced.

You don't necessarily have to make an all-or-nothing choice when it comes to deciding whether to get legal help. You can ask a lawyer to help you by looking over the paperwork that you've prepared yourself to make sure it's properly filled out. The lawyer isn't officially representing you, but is supporting you in representing yourself. Not all lawyers will do this, but some will, and you'll save a lot of money that way. And in some states, you can get help from a paralegal or legal document preparer, who will gather information from you and then fill out your court forms for a few hundred dollars.

RESOURCES

OTHER BOOKS OFFER DETAILED HOW-TO ADVICE ON DIVORCING. For example, *We The People's Guide to Divorce* (Wiley) offers forms and do-it-yourself information for all 50 states, and *Divorce Yourself*, by Daniel Sitarz (Nova), has advice for every state on how to do your own divorce, along with forms on CD. Numerous websites also offer resources for do-it-yourself divorcées: www.divorceinfo.com, www.divorcenet.com, www.divorcecentral.com, and www .divorcesource.com are just a few. General legal sites like www .alllaw.com or www.legalzoom.com can also be helpful. Many of these sites offer links to marital settlement agreement forms and other paperwork that you can use to complete your own uncontested divorce.

Negotiating with Your Spouse

Coming to agreements about property, custody, and support will take a significant amount of negotiation. This is particularly true if you and your spouse decide to do the divorce yourselves, but even if you have lawyers, you will still be involved in negotiating the terms of your divorce agreement. It's important to keep a balance between compromising when it makes sense and feels possible to you, and standing up for what you think is right and fair.

You're most likely to get a good result if you have support: friends and relatives who can coach you through the worst of the legal battles and provide help until the details of the divorce are settled and things return to a calmer state.

True Stories: Difficult Transitions

"All hell broke loose when Lois and I filed for divorce," says Ed. "I sure wasn't prepared to deal with all the crap it brought up. In the middle of the legal stuff, it was really tough going back to the house to pick up the kids and deal with Lois. She was really p-o'ed. So was I, of course. The kids were four and seven then.

"I was living in this loft apartment we'd fixed up over my brother's garage. It wasn't such a bad place, in fact it was pretty nice, but I felt bad about bringing the kids there...and it was always hard dealing with Lois's anger when I went over to pick them up.

I also got into this really ambivalent thing about fighting Lois's lawyer on every little thing. I felt like if I gave in too easily just to placate her, I'd live over my brother's garage the rest of my life. I'd be really resentful and it would affect my relationship with my kids. The short-range problem was the tension of fighting with Lois, and to be honest, this affected how I felt when I was with the kids. I wanted to see my kids, but I sure didn't want to see her. Eventually, I got my sister-in-law to pick up the kids and bring them over.

"The long-range problem, as my brother pointed out, was that if I gave in to all Lois's divorce demands, it would wipe me out clean. I'd end up carrying my regrets and resentment for the rest of my life. For sure that would affect the kids! Eventually we came up with a pretty decent arrangement that both Lois and I could live with—and that didn't damage my future relationship with my kids."

Help From a Therapist

If you're optimistic that you and your spouse can work things out, but you're getting stuck on certain issues, consider finding a therapist who is willing to help you to sort out basic financial and custody issues and reach agreements. Therapists are usually considerably less expensive than lawyers. They offer the added value of possibly helping you process and heal some of the anger you and your ex are probably feeling.

Not every therapist, however, is willing to work on "legal" issues, such as dividing assets or making a custody arrangement. Be sure that when you interview a therapist, you explain exactly what you want from the process. Make sure you let the therapist know that you'd like help sorting out both the emotional and practical issues so that you can find your way to agreements.

Here are some tips for finding a therapist to work with:

- If you have friends who are seeing a therapist, or who have seen one in the past, ask them for recommendations. Remember you're not exactly seeking couples' counseling, so make sure you ask them whether they think the therapist will be able to work with a couple who's not interested in reconciliation, but needs help with post-divorce communication.

- Understand that therapists have specialties. If the phone book is your only resource for finding someone to work with, look under the heading "Marriage & Family Therapists."

- If the first therapist you call isn't willing to take on new clients who are in the midst of a divorce, ask for names of other therapists you might call.

Before your first session, be sure you and your ex get clear with each other about the points you need to cover, and about what is on the list that you need to divide and decide. In your first meeting with a therapist, be very clear about the kinds of help you want. It's a good idea for you to work this out ahead of time. For example, you might say that you are both very clear about wanting the divorce, but that you would like the therapist to guide you along the most peaceful path possible for getting it—including working out visitation rights with the kids, and financial issues. Unless you want to consider reconciliation, make sure you tell the therapist that that isn't what you're there for.

Be prepared for the therapist to ask personal questions about your marriage and/or your own personal history—some of which you might not want to answer. If it is unclear to you how answers to such questions might help you and your divorcing spouse to work out the present settlement issues, ask the therapist to clarify.

If at the end of your first meeting with the therapist, you and your spouse agree that this person is not helpful, or cannot provide you with specific help that you are seeking—for example, help dealing with financial conflicts—seek other sources of help. This might mean trying another therapist or a mediator.

When you've done all you can with your therapist, the next step is to get your agreements in writing. If you've hired lawyers, take the results to them for reality-checking, fine-tuning, and drafting into a document that you can submit to the court as your divorce settlement. If you are proceeding without lawyers, at some point you'll need to make sure your agreements get put into writing in a way that conforms with the laws of your state. You can do this by having a lawyer review the agreement, by asking a legal document preparer to put the agreement into the appropriate form, by using a do-it-yourself book that's applicable to your state, or by using a divorce website that offers marital settlement agreement assistance.

Help From a Mediator

Another option is to hire a mediator to help you work out a divorce settlement. A mediator is a person—often a lawyer, but possibly a therapist—who is trained to help people work through problems outside the courts. A mediator is a neutral person who works directly with you and your spouse, usually together, to help you communicate better and resolve issues that you've not been able to negotiate on your own. A mediator is not a marriage counselor and is not going to help you reconcile, nor will most mediators do the kind of work on trying to heal the relationship that you may find in therapy.

Nor does a mediator—even one who's a lawyer—tell you what to do. The mediator works with you and your spouse directly and simultaneously, and is not allowed to give legal advice to either of you. A mediator may, however, give you information, such as how much a judge might order as child support, or how visitation is likely to be ordered in your local court. The decisions are all in your hands—the mediator just facilitates your decision-making process.

Bring your collaborative stance and your best self to mediation and you'll save a great deal of money and pain. Give it your best try. And at each step of the way, remember that everything you do now helps to define the new relationship that you are developing with your ex-spouse.

Arbitration

Arbitration is becoming increasingly popular in divorce cases as an alternative to court. In arbitration, you and your ex-spouse hire lawyers and take your case to an arbitrator—usually either an attorney or a retired judge—to rule on the issues you couldn't resolve. The arbitrator will listen to each of your attorneys argue and then decide how your property should be divided or how your parenting plan should be structured. Just like when you go to court, you end up with a binding document setting out each person's responsibilities. And just as when you go to court, decisions about support and visitation can always be reopened if circumstances later change. Whenever kids are involved, the courts retain the power to change earlier decisions when there's a good reason.

Arbitration isn't cheap, because you'll each be paying for your own attorney and also for the arbitrator's time. And you give up control of the decision-making process, which you keep when you negotiate a settlement in mediation, therapy, or a collaborative divorce. But it should be a lot faster and less expensive than a court-processed divorce.

The Collaborative Divorce Approach

Collaborative divorce is a process in which you, your wife, and your attorneys commit to resolving all issues of your divorce by negotiated agreement without resorting to, or threatening, costly court proceedings. Collaborative divorce uses informal methods such as open and voluntary disclosure of financial documents, four-way conferences, negotiation, and, when needed, outside professionals such as accountants, financial planners, and family counselors.

While some attorneys may refer to themselves as being "collaborative in style", true collaborative law requires that all parties commit to a "no court" policy: an agreement that if you aren't able to resolve the case with your collaborative lawyers and you want to proceed to court, you will both have to hire new lawyers for the contested court process. This provides a powerful incentive to get the case settled so that you don't have to pay a new lawyer to get up to speed after you've already been through a long negotiation with your first lawyer.

Collaborative divorce is a great middle ground because you and your spouse each have the security of having your own lawyer looking out for your interests, while at the same time, everyone involved in the process has expressed a strong commitment to a negotiated settlement. Collaborative divorce is growing in popularity all over the country, so do some research and see whether there are collaborative lawyers in your community.

RESOURCES

CHECK OUT MEDIATION AND COLLABORATIVE DIVORCE. Two good books that will help you understand mediation and the collaborative process are *Divorce Without Court: A Guide to Mediation & Collaborative Divorce*, by Katherine E. Stoner (Nolo) and *A Guide to Divorce Mediation: How to Reach a Fair, Legal Settlement at a Fraction of the Cost*, by Gary J. Freidman (Workman).

How to Choose an Attorney

There's a saying that sometimes having a good lawyer on your side is more important than having justice on your side. That's cynical, but there may well be some truth in it. You want a good attorney to advise you, negotiate for you and, if it's absolutely unavoidable, fight for you in court.

A good attorney, like a good doctor, is best searched out through personal and professional referrals. Divorce is not uncommon these days, so your friends, family, therapist, or colleagues will probably have leads and recommendations for you. If you have a relationship with a lawyer for business purposes, a good place to start is to ask that lawyer for referrals to divorce attorneys. If you cannot get any good personal referrals, you can contact:

- a local bar association
- a legal aid society, or
- a lawyer's directory (commonly found online, but also in books at your local public library or law library) that tells you something about the experience and qualifications of the lawyers listed.

Many of us, in the midst of the emotion of a divorce, just want someone—anyone!—to lift the burden from us. So there's a tendency to walk into a lawyer's office, lay your troubles on the desk, and say, "Deal with it!" Resist the temptation. Instead, interview your attorney as if you were interviewing a new employee for a business you are running. After all, you'll be hiring—and paying—the attorney, and you need a good idea of whom you're dealing with.

It's wise to visit a few attorneys and find the right fit for you. It is appropriate to ask your prospective attorney for references from other lawyers or former clients. Before you hire anyone, make sure you discuss how important it is not to hurt the kids by being overly aggressive. And don't be afraid to ask questions.

WHAT TO ASK PROSPECTIVE ATTORNEYS

Here are questions designed to elicit substantive responses to consider as you make your final decision:

- How many years of successful experience in divorce cases do you have?

- Are there any new laws that might affect the case? You may be able to tell from their answer whether or not they are keeping up with changes in divorce and tax laws.

- What is your policy about returning phone calls or responding to emails? Let them know that you expect to be informed immediately of any developments in your case and that you expect prompt responses to communications—within 24 hours is usually reasonable.

- Are you comfortable with keeping as our highest goal making my ultimate relationship with my ex-wife and my children cooperative rather than adversarial? Any lawyer who tries to talk you out of this basic principle should be crossed off your list.

If you bring up these issues in your early interview, you'll more than likely get a pretty good picture of your potential attorney. If the lawyer stumbles around, hems and haws, or argues with you about how you are seeing things, forget it and move onto the next interview.

Making a Paper Trail

Whether or not you think that you might be heading for a major contest in divorce court, be prepared. Begin with a paper trail. Keep a journal with dates, times, and outlines of discussions (including phone conversations) you have had with your ex or your attorneys. If you use email to communicate with your ex, keep electronic copies that you could later print out. If you make an oral agreement—anything from dates to pick up the kids to issues as earthshaking as who gets custody of the goldfish—document it with an email saying what you believe your understanding or agreement is. This can be genuinely helpful to both of you, by highlighting misunderstandings early, when they can be easily cleared up.

TIP

BE CAREFUL WITH EMAIL. While it's a good way to make and confirm appointments, or to confirm an agreement you have made or are in the process of making, don't try to deal with potentially contentious issues this way. Andy, a psychotherapist who works with men's groups, recommends, "If it's an emotionally significant issue, at least communicate by phone, if not in person. There's something about email that sometimes flattens emotional content and at other times exaggerates it. Even if both parties have mastery of language, both in listening and writing, I still think it would be a problem. My advice is to use email only if you have pretty objective, nonemotional content to convey."

And don't carry this business of documenting everything to extremes. For example, I've seen people run around with little recorders in their pockets, insisting on taping every conversation with their ex. If you want your relationship to get really tense, I guarantee this will do the trick. But if you are trying to keep your relationship with your ex amicable, be aboveboard and out-front about documenting, and keep documentation within reason.

When You Have to Fight

Situations do exist where you have no choice but to bring issues into court—for example, if your ex is drinking to excess, you may need to change the kids' living situation or ask for supervised visitation. If you have evidence of child abuse or neglect, be sure to get good legal advice. Likewise, if you have good cause to believe that there is a problem with substance abuse or criminal activities, seek legal advice, collect evidence that will hold up in court, and be ready to stand your ground.

Unfortunately, in custody fights it is not unusual for parents to attack and accuse each other, sometimes in the most vicious of ways. If you've got a real battle going on, understand that you could be accused of almost any kind of wrongdoing, including serious neglect or abuse. If this happens to you, stay calm, and no matter what, don't retaliate. There is nothing a judge likes less than parents who fire cross-accusations at each other until no one knows which end is up. Just take whatever steps you need to take in order to disprove the accusations against you, including getting a trained custody evaluator to talk to you, your kids, and your spouse and then make a recommendation. In many disputed custody cases, the judge will order this, but if not, you should make it happen yourself.

At this point, it's probably best to keep the communication indirect, through the attorneys. Don't get pissed off and strike back. You will make the strongest showing in court by spending your time and energy showing that you're reasonable and ethical. You don't make points by alleging the moral decay of others. The judges do not look favorably upon a dad who gets into a hassle, particularly in a courtroom setting. But a demonstration of grace under fire will position you as a stable family leader. This holds true both in and out of the courtroom.

Make it a rule to be entirely truthful in your dealings with your lawyer, your ex, and yourself. It's especially important never to accuse your ex of abuse or neglect unless you know for a fact that it's true—and take a good hard look at your motives before you make any allegations like that. It's distressingly common for one party in a divorce to try to spin a minor human foible into a serious moral issue.

True Stories: Think Before You Speak

Richard accused his ex of being psychotic and unfit to have custody of their only child, who was 16 at the time. The only evidence Richard could offer was that his ex raged at him whenever he showed up at her doorstep, and that she had been like this for years during their marriage. While it was true that Richard's ex raged at him, she was anything but psychotic. She held down a responsible job where she was well-liked, and an investigation by Social Services concluded that she was an excellent mother. Richard's allegations were way off base. They cost him his credibility in court, and his ex ended up winning their custody fight. But more than time lost with his daughter, his actions aggravated tensions between himself, his daughter, and his ex, and years would pass before he could repair the damage he'd done to those relationships.

Whether you end up in a court trial or not, the atmosphere can become highly adversarial even if you and your ex have vowed you wouldn't let that happen. The action that triggers a fight could come in the form of a direct attack from your spouse on your voicemail or email, or an indirect communication from her lawyer to yours about something terrible you've done, recently or long ago. If you feel attacked, invoke the 24-hour rule—that is, don't respond for at least 24 hours.

And before you do respond, talk to your lawyer and set the record straight. It's especially important if you are accused of something serious such as hiding assets, endangering your child, or substance abuse. On the other hand, if an accusation is true, sometimes the best tactic is to agree gracefully that you recognize your actions were less than ideal and move on.

True Stories: The Path of Least Resistance

When things started heating up in Matthew's divorce case his attorney candidly advised him, "Look, on the basis of what you've shared with me about your marriage, I've got to warn you. Your wife won't stop at anything to keep you from getting custody of your daughter. I recommend you back off, let her have full custody. Then make damn sure you're available to your daughter twenty-four hours a day, seven days a week. Give her a cell phone so she can call you whenever she wants. And whenever you have time with her, keep it quality time."

Matthew went home from his attorney's office that afternoon and lay awake all night worrying about what his ex might do. Matthew had had an affair with a woman from his office that he and his ex dealt with in couple's counseling. He had never done anything like that again, but he was still afraid of it being used against him in court, along with a few other things he wasn't proud of—including the very occasional use of recreational pot with friends. While he felt like he was being blackmailed, Matthew decided not to press the issue. Instead, he took his lawyer's advice and went along with the custody arrangement his ex-wife had demanded.

Like Matthew, sometimes you'll need to take the path of least resistance. If you have done things in the past that you are not proud of, don't try to deny them or throw similar accusations at your ex. Own up to your mistakes and do the best you can with the history you have. And even in the face of severe challenges like resigning yourself to having less time with your kids than you want, hold to the rules of collaborative divorce. It may be painful in the short run, but it should also create opportunities for conflicts to resolve over time and for new possibilities—maybe even a change in your custody arrangement—to open up in the long run.

Think Ahead

If you can anticipate potentially harmful allegations your ex might bring against you, talk to your attorney about them so that you can either defuse them or develop a good defense. And, for sure, if there is anything your attorney should know about you before you go to court, put it all on the table. If you have engaged in any activities that are likely to be used against you, go out of your way to inform your lawyer of those vulnerabilities. There's nothing worse than something coming out in court that you haven't told your attorney about. It's inevitably going to hurt you because the lawyer hasn't had a chance to think about how to deal with it. The impact may come in the form of restricted visitation or custody rights, higher support payments, or a bigger bill from the attorneys. So for your own interest as well as basic ethics, be honorable and truthful in working with your lawyer and in dealings with your ex-spouse.

Learn the Meaning of Restraint

Sometimes, in the midst of battle, the very best you can do is to briefly withdraw from the battle in order to regroup, settle down emotionally, and reclaim some semblance of reason. If there are times you can't do this by yourself, talk with a friend or therapist. When we're angry or outraged by the way we've been treated, we tend to get into a very judgmental and externally focused state of mind, fixated on how unjust our adversary is being. While these judgments may be based on more than a grain of truth, dwelling on them only feeds your anger. How do you break out of it? By coming back to your own position, time and time again. And this includes holding strong to your ultimate goal of being as collaborative as you can possibly be—regardless of your ex's actions.

Need a reminder of what collaboration is about? It's basing your decisions and actions on what you can do to serve the highest good. Or, put even more simply and directly, it means keeping the well-being of your kids the top priority. In most cases, compromises will be necessary based on your assessment of what is the highest good possible at this time. In fact, you can count on it. And the as-good-as-you-can-get settlement may be far from comfortable for you.

Nonetheless, put yourself in your ex's shoes whenever you can, even if it's just for the moment. That doesn't mean agreeing with her. It only means taking a few moments to grasp that, at some very basic human level, she is fighting from a place she believes in. No, it may not be just and fair by your book. It may not be reasonable. It may even be vindictive, selfish, or just plain nuts by your way of thinking. But by having some feeling for her experience, you'll be better able to hold your own position, acting in a way that won't get you in trouble and that may ultimately work very much in the favor of you and the kids.

You needn't beat the enemy to the ground to win. In fact, if you look at human history, you'll find that lasting peace is never gained that way. It's gained by tenaciously negotiating in good faith. It helps to have the patience of Job, of course, to keep going forward in search of a settlement. Often, that place of peace is beyond your ability to even imagine. It may even come a year or two or three down the line. That's a difficult perspective to keep in mind, but if you can, it will make things much easier, and may well be the one thing that keeps you and your kids out of a prolonged court battle.

Assume the Impossible Is Possible

While you are negotiating with your ex to work through the legal challenges, you may find that holding collaborative ideals is looking increasingly difficult. In fact, you may be tempted to throw up your hands and say it's impossible. What makes it possible is being as realistic as you can be about goals. Sometimes the highest purpose you can serve is to keep your side of the fight fair and keep the kids and your divorce out of court. As I learned during my divorce, you're mostly putting out fires during the early divorce negotiations. You're keeping down the sparks so they won't burn down to the hidden tinder and ignite a major blaze. If you're the main breadwinner, being fair means coughing up the money to support the kids. It might mean paying over some of your hard-earned savings. And if you're worried about money, the single best thing you can do for yourself is to keep your attorneys' fees down by staying out of court.

When your energy is wearing thin and you're depressed and beaten down, there's a tendency to just cave in and give up. Let them take you to the cleaners. What do you care? Well, don't give up caring for yourself along with the kids. My friend Howard put it well: "What's fair isn't just a money thing. Things got pretty mean in my divorce, and I got so tired of the fight I was ready to give up and give my ex whatever she was asking. Then I realized that if I threw in the towel, I'd be so shredded emotionally and so strapped financially for the next ten years that I'd have nothing to give the kids or anyone else. I'd be a hollow man with an empty piggy bank. I had to pay attention to that. I had to insist on holding onto something I could live with. If I went away wrecked, my kids would never know their dad because I'd be working 24/7 just to cover their support payments, their private school, and their mother's alimony. In the end, I applied for and got scholarships for my kids at the school they'd been attending, and my ex settled for half the alimony she was seeking. But to get that I had to stand up and defend my own truth, though this came at a time when I felt totally wrung out and defeated."

While this may not sound like collaboration on the surface, it is exactly that. Collaboration doesn't mean being a nice guy and giving away everything you've got. It isn't peace at any cost. Your peace must include being there for the kids, and those emotional and spiritual resources need to be honored as much as you honor your bank account.

Don't Underestimate Your Stress

If you and the kids' mom get into big battles in front of the kids, or if you get so out of control that you resort to physical threats, you can end up with a restraining order that prevents you from going anywhere near your children or your ex. You may be a pretty cool-headed guy most of the time, but two acquaintances I consider to be very sane and reasonable men really went over the edge during divorce negotiations. They both ended up enrolling in anger management classes, giving proof to the courts that it was safe to lift the restraining orders their exes got against them. Why am I telling you this? Because many of us don't know how to best monitor our own stress levels. We fool ourselves into believing we're on top of things. And then, the heat suddenly goes up a mere two degrees and we lose it completely.

What are the symptoms that might indicate that you are very close to your boiling point? If two or more of the items on this list apply to you, they are good indications that your stress level is climbing:

- You find yourself using alcohol or other drugs—prescription or otherwise—to feel better.
- You have difficulty sleeping.
- You avoid spending time with friends.
- Your shoulders and back feel tense and stiff, or you have back pain.
- You feel distracted much of the time.
- You are short-tempered with co-workers or friends.
- You spend more time in front of the TV or surfing the Internet.

You might well feel that you're in control and can handle whatever is happening. But now is not the time for being a tough guy. If you feel you're on the edge of losing that last bit of reason you've been clinging to, do something before you blow up. If you're having trouble with anger, look around for a good anger management class. Talk with a good therapist, remembering that therapists are cheaper than lawyers and the long-term gains of spending a few hours with a therapist can be enormous; not always the case with lawyers, even when you win. Collaboration comes in many forms. Chapter 8 has more about taking care of your own emotional state.

Opportunities for Personal Growth

We've all heard that old homily about every challenge in life being a chance for growth. And by now you probably feel that you've completed your graduate work several times over and deserve at least your honorary Ph.D from the University of Hard Knocks. I know that I've felt that way more times than I can count. As I look back on those long years of travail during my divorce, I have to admit that I learned a lot about patience, negotiation, seeking the highest good, and working toward collaborative solutions—more than I ever would have learned elsewhere.

Could I have said it was all for the good at the time it was happening? Well, no. So I probably shouldn't try to convince you of that right now. Nevertheless, take it from someone who's been there and come back with whatever treasure was to be found. Over time, wounds from this period have mostly healed. And, believe me, there were some pretty big ones. Am I grateful for what I had to go through to learn what I did? Well, I wouldn't go that far. But I will say that I'm at peace with myself about those years and, however the lessons came, it's great to have the skills and the wisdom that this difficult time afforded me.

Going through divorce wars is certainly not one of those "opportunities" you go out looking for. But there's no denying—with 20/20 hindsight—that you're going to face major challenges that will force you to develop strengths and abilities you probably never dreamed were within you. Learning to swim with alligators and sharks may not have been your dream in life, but having done so, and survived, you'll carry a knowledge of yourself that will serve you in limitless ways.

Maybe collaboration is ultimately about this anyway—holding a mental picture of something greater than the battle of the moment, and holding your own inner strength regardless of the difficulties. ●

CHAPTER SEVEN

Let's Get Real About the Kids

It seems fair to assume that if you have read this far and have been working to create the collaborative spirit in your divorce, you place your children's happiness and well-being high on your priority list. That's a big part of meeting the challenges of parenting in the context of divorce; genuine caring is at least half of good parenting. Giving your children affection and protection helps to build their emotional security, while age-appropriate and caring guidance teaches self-discipline, the long-term benefits of cooperation, and a balanced sense of responsibility.

> *"If you bungle raising your children, I don't think whatever else you do matters very much."*
> —JACQUELINE KENNEDY ONASSIS

These are all healthy habits. This chapter is about how you can develop those healthy habits and create a functional extended family that includes you, your kids, and your ex.

Becoming the Parent You Want to Be

Within a few months of separating from your wife, you will probably begin to get somewhat settled into your life as a divorced father. While the initial crisis is beginning to fade, you may still be struggling with feelings stirred up by the breakup of your marriage and the need to develop new ways of relating to your ex. Ready or not, it's time to embrace the work of building a positive and forward-looking extended family. You can now turn your attention to being the kind of parent you want to be, creating a new life that supports and nurtures your relationships with your kids.

If you've left a home that was filled with tension and conflict, there can sometimes be a tendency to give a great sigh of relief and then accept whatever comes. I believe we call that "going with the flow." But as a friend of mine recently pointed out, you'd better at least know which flow you're going with. Some of them end up in pure crystalline lakes, some in oceans, and some in....well, you get the point. If your kids are old enough to be out there in the world, they'll be encountering infinite choices, opportunities, and influences, and facing a great many pressures and temptations. This is your opportunity to strengthen or establish your relationships with them so that you can help them to navigate their choices safely and with integrity.

With all this talk about the various problems of fatherhood and building a healthy extended family, it's all too easy to overlook the joys and experiences of deep intimacy and love that are part of raising kids. As you read the guidelines in this chapter, remember that your highest goal is to raise kids who contribute something to the world by being in it, while you enjoy being a father and having your children love, respect, and enjoy being with you.

As a parent, there will be times when you make mistakes and say things you later regret. And being a divorced parent, you'll probably carry around some guilt about your marriage breaking up, along with worry about how the breakup will affect the kids. Regrets are just part of living, and sometimes it seems that having children multiplies our potential for them. As Pete, a single father with the custody of his three children once stated, "If my kids got a nickel for every regrettable thing I ever did raising them, they'd be millionaires. Fortunately for me, they have short memories about all that and they think they've got the best dad in the world. On that count, at least, I try not to dash their illusions."

Although being a caring parent is half the battle, you need specific skills and knowledge, too. It's amazing how many issues come up with growing children that you may have never given too much thought to. Many men begin to discover about this time that they left a lot of those matters to their wives—especially where younger children and "girl things" were involved. If you're planning to have the children with you a lot, you're going to have to learn about these things. In other words, if you're expecting to become more involved with your kids now that you're separated, you may need to bone up a little on parenting skills.

For example, one of the keys of good parenting is knowing what is age-appropriate. Raising competent, skillful, and self-confident kids starts with knowing when a child's body and mind are developed enough to take on a particular challenge. When is your growing child ready to learn difficult, coordinated physical activities, for example, such as catching a ball or riding a bicycle? Each new skill that a child learns requires a specific level of neuromuscular and mental development. If you push them to learn things that require capacities they have not yet developed, they can end up feeling frustrated and incompetent because they're unable to accomplish the things you're asking them to do.

The younger your child is at the time of your divorce, the more important it is to know what is age-appropriate. If you are going to have joint custody and your child is a toddler and not yet toilet trained, what will your responsibilities be? Are you up for it? How will you handle visits when your child is still nursing—and what will the child's diet be like soon after weaning? When is it appropriate to start teaching your youngster to read?

If you have older children, do you know about how to talk with a daughter who is entering puberty and is on the verge of experiencing her first period? And what about your teenaged son's budding interest in sex?

Ask yourself what resources are available to you as you work through these questions. Can you work with your children's mother to learn how to handle these new challenges? Do you need to read some books about childhood development? Is there a family member who's willing to be your counsel and guide? Is there a nearby parenting group (online or off) that you could join? If you think you'll have joint custody of your kids, or even if you're just looking at having them with you on weekends, it would be wise to start lining up people you can call when you have questions.

RESOURCES

 There are plenty of useful books on the subjects of child development and parenting. For example:

Proactive Parenting: Guiding Your Child from Two to Six (Berkeley) by Tufts University's Eliot-Pearson Department of Child Development

The Yale Child Study Center Guide to Understanding Your Child: Healthy Development from Birth to Adolescence (Little, Brown) by Linda C. Mayes and Donald J. Cohen

Ages and Stages: A Parent's Guide to Normal Childhood Development (Wiley) by Charles E. Schaefer and Theresa Foy DiGeronimo

There are also collaborative decisions to be made that will require defining expectations and planning ahead. For example, you've got to set dates for when the kids will be with you and when they'll be with your ex. There may be issues around schooling or religious education that you'll need to work out. Schedules and decisions that may have happened more spontaneously when you were all together in one household might now have to be worked out months ahead, and that means planning.

DIVORCE STORIES: INTENTION MATTERS

Consider the following from C.J., a man who'd been divorced about a year and a half at the time he offered these thoughts:

"The first thing I became aware of after being divorced was how my relationships with my kids were changing. So much of what happened in our family life was my ex-wife June's doing, and I confess I never gave her enough credit for that. She was great at scheduling everything— after-school activities, Girl Scouts, overnights at the kids' friends' homes, camping trips, cookie sales, soccer, doctors' appointments. Me? I was the backup chauffeur.

Since the divorce I've had to give a lot more thought to planning stuff with my kids. I'm taking a much more active role in the decisions and plans. For instance, I believe it's important for them to spend time with just Dad, for us to get to know each other away from all the activities and busyness. I've had to fight for this at times. In all honesty, the changes have made me take a whole new look at how I relate to my kids, not just as Parental Unit #2, as my older daughter refers to me, nor as their chauffeur, either, but as Dad. I'm feeling much more like a parent than I ever did before, when I was married. And mostly I like it!"

Certainly as parents we want to plan our lives so that we can be together and do things with our kids. And we want to help them make good choices and avoid making too many mistakes—especially those mistakes we made ourselves when we were kids! We may also put a high priority on communicating openly and treating each other with care, respect, and love. But these are mostly qualities and values that you can't force-feed. If you do, you'll usually get the opposite of what you had hoped for. These are qualities and values that arise from first building a solid foundation for your relationship.

Building Trust and Accountability

Many children of divorce feel let down and even betrayed by their parents. Years after his parents' divorce, one man, Simon, remembers telling his father, "I hated you for leaving us, and it was the biggest thing in my life to get over your actually moving away to another city. In my mind you were nothing but a big coward." As he grew to adulthood, Simon came to understand his father better. But during his teenaged years, when the boy really needed his father, his dad had truly abandoned him; except for holiday and summer visits, his father simply didn't exist for him. Simon didn't learn his father's side of the divorce, or why he hadn't maintained communication with him, until 20-plus years after the divorce. As a young teenager when his father left, could he have understood his father's position? Maybe not.

When Simon's father finally opened up to him, many years later, he learned two things: first, his dad had been raised to hide his feelings, to never talk about them. And second, the divorce had been precipitated by the fact that his dad's company had transferred him to another city, and his mother had refused to move because she would have had to leave behind the support of her parents and several long-time friends. As an adult, Simon was able to sympathize with what had happened—at least to some degree. But as he said, "If Dad had just been the kind of guy who could talk things over, I would at least have had something more than my own fears and fantasies to battle with. I was like Don Quixote out tilting at windmills, making up enemies that never existed. I was nearly 30 when I learned his side of it, and then my whole view of him changed. Dad has his faults, but don't we all? The point is that he sure isn't the villain I made of him when I was a kid."

From stories like this, we see why it is so important for parents and children to have a relationship where communication is open and where parents' actions are predictable, reliable, and accountable. No matter what the reasons for the divorce were, when you're no longer there to greet your kids when they get home from school or tuck them into bed at night or see their faces when they wake up on Christmas day, they are probably going to feel you've abandoned them. That's the way they might put the story together no matter what the evidence to the contrary.

If you're the parent with primary custody, don't be surprised if the kids wonder why Mom's not with them anymore, and make up stories about that, too. One six-year-old believed that his father had sent his mother away to be adopted by another family. This came about because he had a friend who had been adopted and he got the story a little mixed up. He didn't get straightened out on this until his seventh birthday when he said to his father, "I've got an idea. Let's adopt my mom!"

The stories your children put together around your divorce may or may not coincide with what you know to be true. And you may or may not get the opportunity to correct misperceptions. But the more accountable and open you can be in your daily communications and actions with your kids, the more they will come to see you as a source of security and dependable information in their lives.

"My dad was a psychotherapist," a man in his mid-20s recently told me. "He remarried a couple years after my parents' divorce. Mom was a very difficult person, and Dad and I talked on the phone two or three times a week all through my high school years, mostly about her. He would assure me that Mom loved me. And without ever once putting her down, as far as I can recall, he'd tell me about different things I could try to make things go more smoothly between us. His suggestions didn't always work, but that was okay somehow. I felt I had his support and that he cared enough for both Mom and me to never put her down."

Let the kids know that they are your first priority. This may mean changing the custody arrangement so that the children can feel comfortable and secure, even if it means you can't spend as much time with them as you'd hoped.

KEEP YOUR PROMISES!

I've said this before, and I'll say it again; your primary rule should be: Do what you say you'll do. It's not what you say, it's what you do that teaches the kids where they stand with you. If you promise to take your kids skiing, do it. If you say you're going to show up for their soccer game next weekend, do it. If you've said that they can't watch TV until their homework is done, stick to your guns. Being accountable and trustworthy also means following through on promises they'd rather you'd forget.

Be realistic and make only commitments that you can keep. It's better to promise nothing than to break promises.

> In a workshop, Pierre told us that he'd been divorced for over a year and shared physical custody of his three children. At one point business demands made it impossible for him to be at home every night for his children, so he hired a live-in caregiver. The children were well cared for, but they began phoning their mother anytime they had conflicts with their caregiver. In time, Pierre's ex argued that if he wasn't going to be home for the children, it might be better that they stay with her.
>
> Pierre ultimately agreed to change the custody arrangements so that he had the children only on weekends, because he could not promise to be with them during the week. While the solution wasn't ideal, the children now had a situation that was reliable and dependable. They still didn't see their dad at night but they no longer expected to. On weekends, they could trust that they had his undivided attention. Pierre also made a point of taking the kids to his workplace and showing them around, so that they could feel more a part of this aspect of his life.

Being trustworthy starts with knowing what you can and can't realistically deliver and being honest with your kids about that. "I didn't see my dad often, and my parents weren't even divorced," one man told his parenting group. "He was a sales rep and traveled a lot, including trips to Europe and the Middle East. But he always showed up when he said he would, and when we had time together it was great. Today we're really close and talk on the phone a couple times a week." Generally it's true that the quality of the time you spend with your children—and the quality of your word—counts for a lot.

Keeping Your Kids Out of the Fray

For many of us, it's hard to keep from venting our anger and disappointment about our ex either around our kids or directly to them. You know the riff: "Don't do that. You're acting just like your mother." Or, "Your mother is driving me crazy." Or worse.

I've asked many psychologists why we do this—especially because most of us know better. There are a variety of explanations, most of them not particularly admirable. Sometimes we simply can't contain the anger and frustration we are feeling toward our ex, no matter how much we might try, and it comes out in the process of disciplining our child. Sometimes our child's behavior mirrors something our ex frequently did that caused a great deal of pain. We may know the child doesn't know any better, but our feelings are still raw and we let go with an angry comment we later regret. Or, we're simply having a bad day and anger we're feeling toward our ex slips out and gets misdirected to our children.

Whatever the reason, hearing one parent disparage the other is very confusing and can be extremely upsetting to children. If your parents divorced when you were young, maybe you have firsthand knowledge of how your parents' carping about each other affected you. If not, try to put yourself in your children's place. They love and want to trust both of their parents. But all the bad things their parents say about each other constantly undermine their trust. They may not know what to believe, especially if the bad-mouthing parent's description of the other parent doesn't conform with the child's reality—which will almost always be the case.

One 14-year-old girl, whose parents divorced when she was 12, wrote in an online discussion:

"The very worst thing for me is hearing my mom and dad dissing each other over whatever…it's just anything. It's their thing, I guess. I don't have to listen to it but it's hard to tune out. Sometimes, when I'm feeling really depressed, I hate both of them but mostly I side with Mom, I guess. I just wish she wasn't so friggin' critical of everyone all the time. I think she hates herself and takes it out on everyone. Dad is another story. He takes it out on me….that he has to give Mom a lot of money for me. I'll just be glad when I'm old enough to get out of there, to get a little job somewhere and be on my own. Right now I feel like when I leave I won't even tell them where I go."

Notice that there's no mention of what the parents are saying about each other—that doesn't matter to the teenager who wrote this poignant message. Instead her statement is about how deeply she is affected by her parents' criticisms of each other. She is aware only that they are critical and unpleasant people whose actions cause her pain. While each parent may have been trying to win the girl's loyalty by criticizing the other parent, they ended up undermining their daughter's ability to trust and love either of them. Rather than winning her loyalty, both parents have unwittingly alienated their daughter. I wonder how her parents would feel if they discovered what their behavior was producing—an angry and hurt child who can't wait to get away from them.

However justified you might feel in criticizing your ex in front of your kids, the chances are pretty good that the only messages the kids will really take in are in the tone of your voice, the look on your face, and your body language. These messages will be instantly translated in the child's minds as, "Dad (or Mom) is angry and mean." No matter what your words, they will experience rejection and fear. Some kids will cringe, fearing they might be the next target of their parent's wrath. Others will become focused on figuring out which parent is right and which one wrong. Some will become so conflicted that they will withdraw from both parents and become depressed, while others will reject their parents, believing this is better than being rejected. And still others will become so numbed to their parents' criticisms that they won't hear anything they say.

True Stories:
A Little Intervention Can Go a Long Way

During a peer counseling session, Teri, a 13-year old girl, confided: "Mom and Dad were always telling me about each other's faults and what they'd gone through getting their divorce. I never knew what to say exactly, so I just learned to shut up and get invisible. I got so I was just everybody's mouse and doormat to order around and wipe their dirty feet on. Nobody saw me for who I am or cared that I have a life of my own. That's changed now; thanks to [the peer-counseling advisor] and the stuff I've worked out with these guys [her group]. When my parents start doing that stuff now I tell them that it's between them and none of my business. I tell them I love them both and I don't want to be caught in the middle between their stuff with each other—to just leave me out of all that. It's gotten a lot better since taking that position. I'm my own person now."

Counseling from a therapist or peers can be a great help, but it isn't always available. That's why it's so important for you to recognize signs of stress in your children, to know what you can do to help them cope, and to learn the warning signs that tell you when their stress is becoming serious. (There's more about kids and stress below.)

It's an unusual parent who can refrain from ever dumping their issues with their ex on their kids—it's really hard not to, and it's understandable. Venting out loud usually comes from a place of pain and frustration after years of struggling with an unhappy marriage. But it produces so much harm that you should do everything you can to avoid it—keep in mind the girl who wanted to run away without telling her parents where she was going. The last thing you want is to make your children feel that way.

Parents might do well to remember the old saying from childhood: "Everything you say about me bounces off me and sticks to you!" Rephrase it like this: "Everything I say about my ex bounces off her and sticks to me." Best to keep it to yourself in the first place.

Setting Limits

A lot of divorced dads, especially when visitation time is limited, tend to just want to have fun with the kids. Whoopee! It's party time! However, if you're only going to be a Party Pop, you'll greatly limit your relationship with your children, and you'll deprive them of experiences that will help them grow. Your goal is to create a relationship in which your children can grow into whole people—able to have fun, for sure, but also able to be effective in the world.

In order to help the kids grow and thrive, you'll be called upon to participate in their lives in a number of distinctly non-partying ways, including:

- providing guidance with homework, even if that just means creating and maintaining a quiet study time and a good physical space for them to do their work

- setting limits around behavior and making sure those limits are respected

- developing an appreciation for what it takes to maintain a household by establishing a teamwork approach to daily household chores, including housework, preparing meals, shopping, and doing minor household repairs

- fostering family bonds and communication through eating real sit-down meals together and sharing stories about how things are going in your lives

- overseeing health and personal hygiene such as eating healthy foods, bathing, brushing teeth, and getting exercise, and

- nurturing moral or spiritual awareness or religious education.

Many of these responsibilities on your part may not sit well with the kids all the time, but all of them are a part of developing trusting parent-child relationships that have lasting bonds and integrity—and a part of your children's development into functioning adults. For example, when children are given responsibilities for the daily chores of the household, they learn how their participation truly makes a difference in their own lives and the lives of those around them. They experience their own effectiveness early on. To have a sense of ourselves as capable people, we must experience ourselves as being capable, and that's part of what you can give them by setting appropriate limits and guiding them through their childhoods.

Sometimes They Just Won't Like You

In the heat of a conflict, most of us tend to want to cast things in black and white. That's particularly true of kids, and even more true of young ones between the ages of 5 and 12. An easy first reaction is to look for a good guy and a bad guy—deciding that someone's entirely right and someone's entirely wrong can help explain what happened and why. As a parent, you'll need to prepare yourself for the fact that sometimes you will be assigned the role of bad guy. Maybe Mom tells your teenage son he can't go to a certain concert because you said so. Or your child says Mom said that they can't afford "extras" because you are stingy and don't give them enough money. (You may later discover, of course, that Mom actually said, "Your dad and I don't have a lot of extra money right now, so you'll have to save up your own money to buy that new computer game.")

Sometimes, you'll be the bad guy because you don't give your kids what they want. (This, of course, is true whether or not you're divorced.) Remember that it's your job to set limits, even if it means you fall out of favor temporarily. When you find you're the bad guy, don't try to fix it. Be as direct as possible with the kids about the reasons for your position. For example, you might tell your son, "I know you like to listen to the band called Parked and Ready, but I have heard them, and I don't like what they are putting out. Their attitudes towards women are mean and disgusting. Those aren't attitudes that I can support or that I want my son to support." Once you've had your say, let your kids offer their positions, too. And ask them how you can help them: "I know it's hard to tell your friends your dad won't let you go to the concert with them. Is there a way I might help you to deal with that?" Don't expect them to come up with a mature or appropriate answer to this question. You might suggest, "If it will help, I could talk to your friends and explain why I feel so strongly about this. Maybe we can work this out together."

Without trying to curry favor, you still have a few choices when you and the kids are at loggerheads:

- Try to find trust and friendship in other aspects of your relationship: "Look, I know you like that group Mountain Rush. How about the next time they come through I get you and a friend tickets to their concert?"

- Actively try to educate and influence your child's thinking on the subject: "I'd like for you to think about some of the things that Parked and Ready says about women. Think about how your mother or your sister might feel if you said those things about them."

Lessons like these, which reflect important values you want to share with your kids, will help them to start responding to you as you really are—someone who consistently gives them your unequivocal opinions as well as your love, time, and energy—rather than as some two-dimensional, cardboard model of you. And that's worth spending some time as the bad guy now and then.

Discipline: A Matter of Balance and Control

If there is a single primary goal where disciplining our kids is concerned, it is to teach them to choose well, to be true to themselves, and to hold a life course where their actions and thoughts help them to achieve their fondest dreams and aspirations. Discipline isn't just about having well-behaved kids; its ultimate goal and purpose is to raise kids who have an appreciation for creative and constructive thought and action, with an ability to honor others in the same ways that they honor themselves.

We all want our children to live up to their full potential; in fact, it's a father's duty to help them do exactly this. As the resident role model, you must provide guidance and discipline. But you must also know when to back off. Expecting total control for no reason other than to satisfy your own ego needs can become harmful. One common example of this is the Little League father who places more emphasis on winning than on sportsmanship and having fun. Or consider the stage parent who gets his child into a professional acting career without questioning whether the kid is emotionally mature enough to handle it.

At the opposite pole, some parents are too laissez-faire. They fail to recognize when it's time to step in and exert their authority. They let the child run wild or make inappropriate demands. This is not the time to feel guilty about the divorce and worry that setting limits might make the child not want to spend time with you. Most children innately know that setting limits and demanding reasonable behavior indicates that you truly care about them—even if they get angry at first. Demand acceptable behavior from them and they will come around.

Even a 16-year-old, who can make complicated rational decisions, still usually suffers from naivete and lack of experience in the world. Without reasonable parental guidance they can get into trouble. In the end, if you let a child walk all over you, you'll rarely get the love and respect you crave from that child. Adam, looking back on his own childhood growing up with a father who was very clear and assertive about demanding good behavior, admitted, "Dad's iron hand saved me the embarrassment of submitting to peer pressure to do things I knew weren't right. I could just tell my friends that my father would kill me if I did this or that."

The good magic happens when you strike the right balance between insisting on certain standards and taking a live-and-let-live position. Whenever you come to loggerheads with your kids, work with them to create a win-win outcome. Remember, however, that you can't determine what's a win for them. In other words, the win has to be perceived that way by both of you. To determine that, you have to listen to them and understand when they feel like they are winning.

Jeffrey and his son Marco came to loggerheads over a concert Marco wanted to attend. Jeffrey felt that this band's lyrics demeaned women. He refused to give Marco permission to attend the concert and offered to go with him to a concert that same weekend by a group they both enjoyed. "Dad," Marco said. "Nobody goes to concerts with their parents!" What seemed like a win-win to Jeffrey clearly wasn't a win-win for Marco. Jeffrey listened to his son's concerns, however, and they worked something out. They settled on a concert that Jeffrey approved of and that Marco was delighted to attend with his friends. To sweeten the pot, Jeffrey bought his son the ticket so it wouldn't come out of the boy's allowance.

What Works and What Doesn't

Styles of discipline are as individual as the people who practice them. Do what works for you, but always remember that in anything you do you are modeling behavior that your child will copy and mirror back in relationships with you and others. A child who experiences harsh and painful punishment will often inflict similar punishment on others; this could be a sibling, his friends, or even you and your ex-wife.

The message you want to get across to your kids is simple enough. You want to point them in the direction of acting in ways that will get them what they truly want and will benefit them in the years to come by helping them to function easily in the world. What you don't want is to create an ongoing power struggle. You want your interventions to achieve the following:

- They should have a positive emotional impact on the child.
- They should send a clear message that you are in control of the situation.
- The positive results should far outweigh the negative.
- They should allow both of you to forgive and move on.

Whatever disciplines you impose, children need to be able to predict the consequences of their behavior. Be as consistent as possible. Define your expectations by writing down your rules in simple language and periodically going over them with your children. Post the rules and expectations on the refrigerator door or some other place that both you and your kids can have access to. When there's a violation of the written rules, ask the child to recall that rule. If there is any doubt, read it back from the list. You can point out that it's understandable to forget the rule for the first couple of times but after that, you expect the rule to be honored. If your child doesn't take responsibility, then you will have to do it for him—and the child might not like the way you take responsibility, especially if it affects privileges.

By clearly tying consequences to established rules, you're teaching your child not only to obey the rules, but to take responsibility for making choices. After all, one of the key understandings of any social order is that society demands a certain level of responsibility on the part of every citizen, and when those responsibilities aren't met, society will either punish the violation or demand retribution. As one father put it, "We need to learn that we have a choice—either we take responsibility for our own actions or someone else will! And when it's the latter, we have lost control of our lives."

Control the Consequences

Some parents offer their children the chance to choose in advance what the consequences of their actions will be. Be very careful of this. An example is when a child's punishment involves doing extra chores around the house. Experienced parents will tell you that most children will procrastinate as long as possible, sometimes with the hope that if they delay long enough they'll wear you down and get out of having to do what they've been asked to do. Suddenly, a consequence that you have initiated becomes a whole new game, called let's get out of it. And guess what? You're the one being played in this game. So choose wisely and avoid choices that get you into power struggles with children. Or as a child psychologist friend of mine recently advised, "Pick your battles so that you'll never lose."

What's a battle that you can't lose? If your son has his own phone, take it away for a week. Does your daughter have car privileges? Take away her key. Are there special programs the kids like to watch on TV? Well, too bad.

The TV is off limits. The more immediate the consequences, the better for everyone. Provide your child with minimal opportunities to change the rules on you—and take care that you don't create consequences that you can't live with. If you ground a child for two weeks, that means you become his jailer, and you had better be willing to stand guard 24 hours a day, seven days a week. Is this how you wish to spend your time? Probably not.

Kids, especially younger ones, experience time very differently than adults do. Next weekend can seem like next year or forever in your child's mind. Imagine if you were told that you would be punished for the rest of your life, no matter what you did to make up for it. There'd be no point in trying to be good, would there? It's much better to keep the punishment brief and swift, served out within the same time period that the offense occurred, or at least within a couple of hours or days. In that way, you and your child can move on to the fun things in your relationship. Nobody wants to mope around all grumpy for hours or days waiting for the consequences.

LETTING GO WHEN IT'S OVER

So you've decreed a penalty for your child's unacceptable behavior. The more you think about what they did, the more upset you become. Pretty soon you find you are defining your child in the light of this bad behavior, and seeing them as just plain bad. Be careful. You are skating on very thin ice, and probably behaving in ways that will only reinforce their bad behavior. What you hold in your mind can easily become a self-fulfilling prophecy. You want your child to have an image of him or herself as a really great kid who sometimes—like all the rest of us, including his or her parents—strays from the path. So the moment your kid is back on track put all the discipline stuff behind you. Drop it. You have great kids; focus on that. Let them know that you love them, believe in them, and think they are the greatest.

Teaching Integrity

Integrity is the state of actually being what you present yourself to be—walking your talk. It is not easy to maintain, especially during times of stress. Still, it is important to do well on the integrity front whenever you possibly can. Some people subscribe to the "don't do as I do, do as I say" school of parenting. This is very confusing to children, who can see that you act in ways that you have tried to teach them are unacceptable. "My old man used to whip my butt for using a curse word," one young father told me, "but when it came to his own mouth, forget it. He cursed like a drunken sailor. When I was a senior in high school, I got a rep as a con man and liar. Nobody could trust a word I said. I think it was my own twist on what old Dad taught me. Say whatever you think will get you what you want—any means to an end. I still find it difficult to stay on track with my deepest convictions because, on first glance, everything just looks like another lie to me."

Learning integrity, learning to walk your talk, is an important practice. Disciplining yourself to live by your values and beliefs every moment of the day is one of life's greatest challenges. But the rewards are great, allowing you to feel more centered and whole and more focused in your purpose. It's this wholeness that will deeply impress your own children, teaching them how to create lives of their own that are happy and intentional.

"But Mom Said I Could!": Collaborative Discipline in Two Households

At first, you can expect some difficulties for everyone in adjusting to having two households with the kids shifting back and forth. For a while, it will definitely be tough on everyone—but most veterans of the single dad lifestyle will tell you that in time everything will settle down. In the meantime, you may get tired of hearing, "But that's not how we do it at Mom's!"

If you're anything like me, you'll probably get irritated if your children's mom tries to tell you how to discipline the kids. Well, rest assured that the reverse is also true. Unless there is a serious case of abuse or neglect going on—or unless your ex asks for your help—it's usually best to leave well enough alone and honor each other's domain. Instead of telling her how to run things, focus your attention on what you do when the children are in your home. Make your rules abundantly clear to your children. Getting your kids to honor the rules no matter whose home they're in teaches a much more positive lesson than does a series of power struggles with your ex about whose system is right.

Still, while you need to create you own house rules and family rituals and let your ex run things her way in her home, your kids can get caught in the middle at times. There may be a dozen little things they complain about, but one thing that will often lead to conflict is if one of you is much more permissive than the other. You may get cries of unfair treatment for a long time to come if your ex and you don't uphold some consistent limits.

The first step in collaborative parenting is for you and your ex to find out whether there are rules that you can share, to give the kids a sense of consistency. Not every rule really even matters that much, but some may be important for the kids, and some may need your collaborative participation. For instance, if your ex has forbidden your kid from associating with a particular friend, find out why. Her position might require your full support. This isn't about your friction with her; it's about creating a healthy, secure, and somewhat predictable environment for your children, so that they can feel there is some continuity between their two homes.

True Stories: Working Together

For years before they were divorced, Bart and his wife, Kathy, fought over raising their two teenaged sons. In fact, as Bart said, "the behind-the-scenes bickering about what we should demand of our kids probably contributed a lot to our split-up." Bart now admits the problem was often that he really dug in his heels on many issues that wouldn't have been so important to him if Kathy hadn't refused to follow through on any of the rules he tried to establish. For example, he insisted that when the boys played music in their rooms that they keep the decibels within a reasonable range. That meant that he didn't want to have to hear their music when he was reading or watching TV. Kathy didn't enforce the rule, so Bart was always the bad guy insisting that they turn the music down, while Kathy got to be the cool mom who didn't make a fuss.

When Bart moved out, all hell broke loose in the house. The boys literally took over and, unable to control them, their mom retreated to her room. After three months of this, she called Bart and asked for his help, explaining what was happening. Bart was tempted to say, "I told you so," but being a good collaborator, he didn't stoop so low. Instead, he told her to put the boys on the phone, and he read them the riot act. He told them that he didn't expect to hear any more complaints about their behavior. They were grown up enough to know exactly what they were doing. As their dad, he expected them to treat everyone, but especially their own mother, with respect and a sense of fairness. After all, they didn't play loud music when they came to his house, and everyone was happier with that arrangement.

Bart had to repeat this lecture more than once—in time, the boys settled down, but Kathy had to call Bart two or three times a week for a while to convince the boys that even though their dad lived in a different house, he was still their father and a force to be reckoned with in terms of discipline. In Bart's case, it was the first test of his collaborative intentions and he learned a lot from it—including how his own stubborn reaction to Kathy's more lenient position on discipline had contributed to conflicts in their marriage.

Even with a basic level of collaboration, you will probably find that you and your ex simply do certain things differently. If it's very important to you, stick to your guns about how something needs to run in your household. You can say to your kids, "I know your Mom has different rules in her house. She and I have talked about it. But when you're here with me, both your mom and I expect you to honor my rules." To be truly collaborative, make an arrangement with their mom that you each will let the kids know that you expect them to abide by the standards of whichever house they are in.

The kids will eventually realize that their resistance is useless. You and their mom are just different people, and there's nothing wrong with that. In fact, both parents are respecting each other's differences and are expecting the kids to honor those differences as well. Giving them the chance to come to terms with such realities is ultimately a good thing. It will provide them with a solid foundation for accepting and encouraging diversity of thought and experience.

Don't be surprised if your children engage in little games of "divide and conquer." If they don't get their way with you, they may go to their mom and get what they want from her. This is standard operating procedure for children, whether or not their parents are together. If your ex is inclined to indulge the children in ways you are not inclined to, there may not be a great deal you can do about it.

True Stories: The Apple Never Falls Far from the Tree

Were you imagining things, or did your kid just act exactly like your ex? Don't be surprised. You may be seeing things in your child that remind you of things you didn't like in your ex—or maybe even that you don't particularly like in yourself. Kids are great at mirroring their parents' best and worst traits and habits. Some of these traits skip around in the family, so maybe your child does something that reminds you of one of your own siblings or the child's grandparents. While these similarities can be a source of wonder, they can also be a source of conflict for you, echoing traits that you did not enjoy in your ex or in some other member of your family.

When Tyler divorced, he became concerned when he noticed how much of his daughter's behavior was like her mom's. "I have to say," Tyler explained, "Sonja is as stubborn and bull-headed as her mom. We get into it at least once every weekend she stays with me, and it's like being married to her mother all over again."

Tyler was locking horns with his daughter in much the same way he once had with his wife. He eventually did some work with a psychotherapist who helped him with this. "I was having one hell of a time with it," he explained. "Whenever Sonja and I got into a conflict it opened up old wounds and I found myself diving right into unfinished business with my ex. I had to take a close look at my own stuff and what I contributed to the problem. I eventually saw that Sonja is her own person and my issues aren't with her. When she gets into a stubborn streak, I can now address it as her and only her behavior, not all mixed up with the crap between her mother and me. And since I have been facing some of my own demons, it's going a lot better between my ex and me."

As he progressed in his understanding of how to deal with his daughter's stubborn behavior, Tyler noticed that Sonja and her mother were also having problems. They each complained about the other's stubbornness—the very same trait that they themselves were most guilty of. While Tyler could see what the problem was, he could do little about it, given that his ex didn't exactly seek out his opinion on such things. However, he still had a friendly relationship with his ex's brother, who also had noticed what was happening with his sister and his niece. That brother eventually stepped in to help mother and daughter resolve it.

Watching for Signs of Stress in Your Kids

Divorce is on every psychologist's list as one of the biggest stressors of human life; short of living in a war zone, it's considered one of the most traumatic events you can go through. For kids, especially younger ones, it represents a critical rent in the fabric of their worlds. As one woman put it, reflecting on the divorce of her parents when she was 12, "It pulled the cosmic carpet right from under my feet and I found myself flailing around in space all through my adolescence."

Although divorce can be painful and scary, large numbers of children live with it, get through it, and end up doing just fine. It's both predictable and healthy for your kids to experience sadness, anger, anxiety, and insecurity during this turbulent time. Most of the time, they'll develop effective mechanisms to deal with those feelings. Your job is to provide a stable and loving home and to use your good judgment about when to line up special help.

To help your children, learn to recognize the signs that tell you when your kids are stressed out and struggling. Don't think that just because your kids seem fine, they really are. Pay attention to signals that all is not well, and act on them quickly.

Kids Stress Differently than Adults

Kids express their emotional difficulties differently than most adults do. Symptoms of adult depression can include alterations of usual sleep patterns, increase or decrease of appetite, mood swings, decreased energy, lowered sex drive, and lack of interest in the world around them. A depressed child may also have changes in sleep patterns or appetite, but will also act out in other ways—possibly getting belligerent or even combative or aggressive, rather than turning inward as adults tend to do.

Of course, kids are individuals, and each responds to stress in unique ways.

Signs of Stress in Younger Kids

There are different challenges for you as a parent at each level of development for your kids. Very young kids, in particular, can't communicate their feelings verbally, so you need to be attentive to their behavior. Here are some things to look for.

Under Age Two

- not wanting to eat or nurse (particularly foods they ordinarily like)
- crying more than usual
- becoming irritated by seemingly small things, and
- changing sleep patterns.

Preschoolers from two to five

Note that some of these behaviors are typical of children this age—that's why the list says to be alert for changes, increases, or an unusual degree of the behavior.

- diminished appetite
- unusual anger when things don't go exactly their way
- stomachaches, headaches, increased infections such as colds or earaches
- sleep problems such as not wanting to go to bed at night or for naps, waking up during the night, and increased nightmares
- being more clingy or whiny than usual
- regression in toilet training—having more accidents, not wanting to use the potty, bedwetting
- babytalk, sassing, and/or not wanting to talk or answer questions they are asked, and
- crying or pouting to an unusual degree when they don't get what they want.

Elementary School Children

May have symptoms similar to preschoolers, and also:

- problems with their friends or teachers
- refusing or resistanting participating in activities
- trouble applying themselves to schoolwork or concentrating on simple tasks
- difficulty getting to sleep at night, or waking in middle of night
- increased number or duration of infections, such as colds and upper respiratory infections, or earaches, and
- bed-wetting as a new or recurring problem.

If you notice any of these symptoms in your child, monitor them. Here are some of the things you can do to help your young children cope with their stress:

- Do whatever you can to spend more quality time with them, cuddling, reading a story together, going on an outing they particularly enjoy, and listening to what they have to say and responding in reassuring ways.
- If they are going to be confronted with a stressful situation, such as going to the dentist or to the doctor, especially for shots, prepare them by letting them know about it ahead of time and assuring them it will be okay (and perhaps promise them ice cream afterwards).
- Take more time with them at bedtime, or during naps, so that they feel comfortable about going to sleep.
- Talk with them about feeling "stressed," or being uncomfortable in their daily lives; let them know that sometimes it's okay to feel scared or lonely or angry.
- Try to anticipate why your child might be feeling stressed and talk to them about it. For example, you might say, "I know you're a little scared about going to the doctor. Let's have a little talk about that, so you can tell me what feels scary to you. It really is going to be okay, you know."

When a child's stress is caused by events that will soon pass, the symptoms of stress will also pass. But if symptoms persist way beyond the time when the source of the stress has passed, it's wise to discuss it with your child's pediatrician. And don't be afraid to seek professional help for your child, even at an early age.

Signs of Stress in Teens

In theory, teenagers should be easier to deal with because they have more reasoning and verbal skills. The problem is, much of the time they don't want to share their feelings or communicate with you at all—it's part and parcel of being a teen. Many kids just want to be with their friends when they're stressed out, while others isolate themselves in their rooms and play video games or read books all day long (or you may not be lucky enough to know what they're doing). There are kids who burn off their stress with lots of activity and exercise and others who turn into couch potatoes, their eyes glued to the TV.

Under stress, teens tend to develop tunnel vision, narrowing their range of interest and activity. This can often pass for the child becoming more disciplined, but the danger is that, given enough stress, kids narrow their horizons rather than expanding them, limiting their development. If your daughter is a high achiever and she starts spending significantly more time studying, that could be a healthy increase in her interest in a particular subject—or a warning sign that she's stressed out and trying to overcompensate. Similarly, if your son begins turning more and more of his attention to extracurricular activities such as soccer or other sports, recognize that this could be a symptom of stress, and check it out.

The bottom line is that you know your kids best. If you have a child who tends to be sensitive and anxious, you'll deal with him or her differently than a child who is generally happy-go-lucky. You need to pay attention to your kids' stress responses and make sure they're within acceptable limits for that particular child. You're not going to keep them from experiencing stress or from acting out in response.

Dealing with Red Flags

What level of stress response in your teenagers is to be expected, and what is simply too extreme? Here are some markers that can help you make that distinction, and some advice about how to deal with them. Apply them with the knowledge that only you have about what your kid is actually like.

- **FALLING GRADES:** It's common for grades to drop some during the throes of a divorce, but if they fall off a cliff and the child is in danger of failing, definitely step in and talk with your child's teacher and guidance counselor. Find out what's going on at school and get suggestions for what you might do.

- **ACTING OUT, CONDUCT PROBLEMS, AND DRUGS:** Teens act out in a variety of ways, from misbehaving at home or at school to experimenting with drugs or alcohol. If the misbehavior is fairly mild or the substance use is merely experimentation, you may be able to intervene yourself to stop it by making it clear to your child that these actions are unacceptable, and placing consequences on them. However, if your child is engaged in criminal activity, or struggling with a serious emotional trauma, extensive drug use, or an onset of mood disorders such as depression or bipolar disorder, seek professional help. Addiction is a serious illness, endangering physical and psychological health and the ability to work or go to school, and it destroys intimacy. If drugs or alcohol are an issue, you and your child should see a mental health professional. Involvement in a 12-step program, or similar peer-run recovery group, may also be helpful. And right away, learn as much as you can about the situation and spend a lot more time with your child, talking with him or her whenever you are together. It's common for a teen who is getting into trouble to be sullen and uncommunicative—don't be discouraged. Try arranging more family outings, and continue to communicate your love and support to your child, without expecting feedback or reciprocation.

- **HANGING WITH A BAD CROWD:** Whom does your child associate with? Do you know his or her friends? If you do not pay attention, you are likely to get blindsided some day soon by trouble you didn't see coming. Your intuition about your kids' friends is one of the most important tools you have. Should your child be mixed up in a truly bad crowd, you will probably find yourself in the unenviable position of trying to control your child's social life. You may want to begin by telling your kid that you are concerned about the people he's spending time with and you want him to stay away from that crowd. More often than not, you're going to have a rebellion on your hands, but be as clear and honest as you can. Let him know that you are concerned, and that you are not arbitrarily trying to restrict activities or friendships. Explain why you think it's important that he find different friends to spend time with, and give him the opportunity to accept the change. Even if he says he will modify his behavior, be very wary until you actually see the promised change.

If your teen refuses to cooperate, you may be in the position of being forced to resort to more severe disciplinary actions. If your child is getting close to adulthood, you may be forced to let go, often to watch him or her continue to make bad decisions. Many older children go through rather dark times, when you feel they are completely lost to you. But just as many come back around, for no particular reason that you can discern. Children, after all, have their own lives, and most are far more resourceful than most parents can imagine.

The trick is knowing when you need to get some intervention for your child, or for your entire family. You need to be especially vigilant if there's a family history of personality disorders, abuse, or other psychiatric problems. Even if these past problems are resolved, it is possible for a child to get into serious emotional trouble when stressed. If you see signs of what you know is real pathology, get your child evaluated by a mental health professional. If you're unsure, go in for a consultation yourself and discuss what you've seen and whether it requires intervention.

Our Teenagers, Ourselves

Being a teenager in today's world isn't easy. Being the father of one isn't either. In fact, many dads concede that raising a teenager is one of the most complicated and challenging experiences they've ever faced. In the teen years, kids are learning how to handle changing roles, moods, and physiology. At one moment, they are testing limits and experimenting with independence. The next, they are seeking closeness and reassurance from their parents that they are still valued members of the family. Teens can also experience great loneliness, and at the same time intense peer pressure to embrace new personal relationships. In the midst of all that, fathers have to learn how to manage and nurture their changing son or daughter.

In his book *Live-Away Dads: Staying a Part of Your Children's Lives When They Aren't a Part of Your Home* (Penguin), William C. Klatte points out that children with little or no contact with their fathers are more likely to drop out of school and become involved in drug and alcohol abuse; girls are more likely to become pregnant as teens, and boys are more likely to become involved in crime and violence. If you weren't already concerned about it, these facts should alert you to the importance of being present in your kids' lives. Here are concrete steps you can take to stay connected to your kids during the teen years.

- **PARTICIPATE IN WHAT YOUR TEENS ARE DOING AT SCHOOL AND OUTSIDE OF SCHOOL.** This includes helping with homework, keeping in contact with their teachers, watching or playing sports together, taking them to see movies or plays that they'll enjoy, planning a camping trip, or simply eating out together.

- **BE AVAILABLE WHEN YOUR KIDS WANT TO TALK.** Whether they want to chat about the good, the bad, the sad, the bewildering, or even the mundane, don't say "in just a minute," or "not right now." Often listening carefully to the emotional content of your kids' questions and trying to link it to something you've felt is the best way to connect. You might tell them, "I only know what I do when I feel the way you're describing." And then tell them a truth about yourself. At the very least, they will understand they are not alone in what they feel, and often that brings the only comfort they need.

- **REGULARLY ASK YOUR CHILDREN ABOUT THEIR LIVES AND THEIR FRIENDS.** Know what fashions, music, television, and movies interest them. As they get older and begin thinking about such things, ask them about their hopes and dreams for the future, and what they'd like to see changed in the world.

- **SHARE STORIES.** Foster your teenagers' courage, integrity, leadership, curiosity, and concern by sharing stories of how you or others have overcome challenges, pursued areas of knowledge that were difficult, or given of yourself to help others. Teach them the joys of succeeding, but also support them when they fail, letting them know that both are part of life.

- **BE CONSISTENT, INVOLVED, AWARE, STABLE, AND NURTURING.** Show up and show interest in what your kids are doing regularly, not just on special occasions.

- **AVOID PUT-DOWNS, JUDGMENTAL TONES OF VOICE, AND UNFAIR GENERALIZATIONS THAT SHOW YOU'RE SIMPLY NOT LISTENING.** Be gentle and nonreactive when you're talking with your kids, and remember that they take in everything you say—not just about them but about the world around you.

- **RESPOND TO YOUR TEEN'S FRUSTRATING BEHAVIOR BY TAKING POSITIVE ACTION, AND KEEP AN EVEN TEMPER.** Always look for the win-win solution.

- **CRACK THE CODE.** Part of being a teenager is having a peer-centered language. You may, at times, feel your teens are talking in code. And you'll probably be right! Committing the time to learn the language will be a relationship-builder. You do this by listening to their words when they are talking with their peers, by listening to their music, and by asking teachers or other parents the meaning of words or phrases you don't understand.

As Teen Sons Mature

It is all too easy, in the busy day-to-day routine of life, to overlook how important fathers are as role models for their teenage sons. Even when he is pointedly ignoring you or rolling his eyes about how uncool you are, your teen son is watching you closely to learn about being a man, how to handle relationships and friendships, and what his role in society might be. If you expect your son to be socially responsible—to obey speed limits when driving or not to take advantage of others—he needs to see you doing the same. Show him how to treat others with respect and to embrace ethical and caring values. Also look at ways he might handle more traditional aggressive roles—for example, to know that when he is verbally attacked by another person it does not need to turn into fisticuffs.

If you want him to be the kind of teenager with whom another father would be happy to send his daughter out on a date, then talk to him about how to behave respectfully towards women. If he's already seen you being respectful of your ex, he has a pretty good idea of this already, but it can't hurt to remind him. And this doesn't just mean the big things, like being responsible about sexual activity. You can also help him learn to be polite, straightforward, and honest, and to resist peer pressure to objectify and demean girls. Modeling is great, but clearly stating the values that underlie your actions will also help your son to grow into the kind of man you want him to be. The same is true for helping your son to resist the temptations of drugs and other high-risk activities.

How you teach your son will also have a lot to do with what kind of kid he is. If he's scholarly and introverted, you may need to help him learn self-confidence and how to be social with others. If he's handsome, popular, and a star athlete, you may have to teach him humility and compassion. The teenage world can be brutal, and you're in the best position of anyone to counteract the lessons that your son will be learning at school, whether they are that he's a nerdy loser or that he's untouchable.

Ask your teen what you can do to be more accessible when he needs to talk. If he doesn't know how to answer this—and he may not—ask other parents what they do, and seek outside resources like parenting groups and books.

As Teen Daughters Mature

For a father, dealing with a teen daughter can be a real challenge. A young daughter will most likely be the apple of dad's eye. As your daughter grows into a teenager, your relationship with her will change. She may no longer like the hugs and cuddles she enjoyed as a young child. She is learning to live in a new body and needs her personal space. Respect this as well as her growing need for privacy, and act in a caring manner that shows her you still love her even as your relationship is changing.

There may be some parts of your daughter's growing up that you'll have to leave to your ex, or to female friends who can be there for your daughter. For example, what will you do if your daughter has her first period while she's staying with you? Most likely she's going to want to talk to a grownup woman who can guide her through this experience. Make sure your ex is ready for the phone call about this, or that you have a female friend who you know your daughter trusts, who can step in. The same may be true of other "female stuff," like going to the gynecologist or shopping for "feminine products." You'll have to figure out how to strike a balance—you need to show that everything that's happening is perfectly fine, and that you're comfortable with all of it, and at the same time you need to give your daughter space and let her talk to whomever will be most comfortable for her. Good luck! If you can manage it, you'll be the greatest dad ever, and your daughter will learn some important lessons.

The teenage years, especially the transition into being a teenager, can be a time when girls start to stress about body image, weight, and appearance. They can sometimes also lose interest in topics that interested them before, like math and science, as they begin to be socialized into more feminine roles. You have a great opportunity to support your daughter's growth by letting her know that her body is fine at any size, and by encouraging her to pursue whatever topics interest her. It's also been shown that participation in sports is very healthy for girls, teaching them self-confidence and contributing to their later success, so if your daughter is inclined that way, give her your full support.

Most fathers are anxious and protective when their daughters begin dating. And it's important to teach your daughter that she shouldn't do anything because of peer pressure or pressure from a boyfriend. When she does begin dating, be watchful, but allow her to make up her own mind about her relationships. And listen to her when she needs someone to talk with. Like your son, your daughter will learn about positive male-female relationships by seeing you acting in a caring and respectful way to her mother, to her, and to any other women in your life.

It's 10 P.M.: Do You Know Where Your Kids Are?

The kids are at their mother's. She's in charge now. You're thinking, "What good does it do me to even worry about them right now? I can't do anything about it." Right? Well, regardless of whose responsibility they are at any given moment, you're going to hear about it if they're getting into trouble. If you're smart, you'll keep in touch—lightly and in a friendly way—wherever they may be. That doesn't mean hovering over them or calling your ex every day for a report on the kids. Instead, a phone call now and then to just chat with your kids, let them know that you are there for them, and that you love them, is a great way to keep in touch when you're not with them. You'd be surprised how much you can learn in this way.

TIP

CONSIDER PAYING FOR A CELL PHONE FOR YOUR KIDS. That way, you can make regular contact without having to involve their mom. Of course if you and your ex have a positive collaborative relationship, you may not mind—the regular contact can also help you to support each other in supporting the kids.

Your goal in keeping tabs on your kids is not to control what they do. Rather, it's to stay close enough with them to catch developing problems early, presumably when they are easier to solve. Remember, you're dealing with teenagers here. In today's world, adolescent culture is a very powerful emotional influence on every teenager. While you can't protect your kids completely, you may be able to either prevent or ameliorate serious problems such as pregnancy, addiction, and accidents. In the process, you can also help your kids grow into healthy, happy, loving, confident, and successful adults. ●

Keeping Yourself Together

Remember the little speech the flight attendant gives when your plane takes off from the airport? Should we lose cabin pressure, oxygen masks will drop in front of you. If you are traveling with a child or an adult who might need assistance, secure your own mask before helping others with theirs.

On the surface, it sounds pretty self-serving to take care of yourself before helping others. But in a depressurized cabin 20,000 feet in the air, one can lose consciousness quickly—or at the very least become disoriented or panicked from the lack of air. If you are going to be helpful, you'd better first make sure you are not at risk yourself.

> *"Each of you is perfect the way you are... and you can use a little improvement."*
>
> —SHUNRYU SUZUKI, ROSHI

You can apply the same principle in times of family crisis. If you are floundering, you will be in no position to help your children. To be their strength and their morale-booster during this time, you will have to be pretty solid within yourself. So taking the time to care for yourself isn't a luxury or a personal indulgence, it's a necessity.

How do you do this when there may be seemingly endless demands on your time and resources? This is "triage" time, and you'll need to prioritize the tasks and responsibilities you're faced with. It's time to sort out what absolutely needs to be given top priority; what can wait until the top priorities are served; and what you can let slip, if need be. In other words, choose your problems rather than thinking you have got to get them all done at once.

Unless you're the reincarnation of Superman, Gandhi, and Mother Teresa rolled into one, your divorce—and especially the period right after you and your wife separate—will feel overwhelming at times. You're getting used to living alone in a new place. You might be working more than one job. Money problems are accumulating, your kids are acting up, you have some kind of conflict with your ex nearly every day, and your girlfriend just dumped you because she thought you were too melancholy. When my friend Jeff found himself in this place, two months after moving into an apartment on his own, he remarked, "I told myself, cheer up. Everything that could go wrong already has. What more could possibly happen? Guess what? The transmission went out on the used car I'd just bought for $3,500, and it cost me $2,200 to replace—which I had to put on a credit card." Eventually things did turn around for Jeff and life settled down, but he seemed destined to hit bottom first. This may be your experience, too, or something very similar. If so, keep in mind that things really will get better—and that no matter how it feels sometimes, you aren't alone.

Recognizing and Managing Stress

There's no getting around the fact that there's a huge amount of stress in the first months of a separation. Recognizing and managing it is the name of the game. Denying that you are under stress is not only unhealthy but as unrealistic as pretending that you can flap your arms and fly. If you're not doing something to minimize the load, any efforts to collaborate are going to turn into battles—either with yourself or with your loved ones, and maybe both. There are endless challenges to be met if you are going to handle things collaboratively with your ex-spouse, challenges that will call on you to be your best self at a time when you probably feel as far from that as you ever have.

Physicians have various tests for rating stress levels related to major life events. Divorce and marital separation generally rate way up at the top of the list, second only to death of a spouse or loved one. On many stress charts, separation from a relationship partner is rated even more stressful than going to jail! In addition to these, high-end stressors include change in financial status, change in the number of marital arguments, change in residence, change in social activities, change in sleeping and eating habits—all of which can go along with separating from your spouse.

STRESS RAISES ITS UGLY HEAD AND SMIRKS: HOW TO RECOGNIZE IT

In order to manage stress you first have to recognize it. In modern world, where stress is just a way of life, we've become so good at pretending it isn't there that most of us don't even know what to look for. If you find yourself suffering from four or more of these symptoms, your stress levels are over the top and it is time to look at what you can do to manage them:

- backache or muscle tension in shoulders, neck, chest or limbs
- elevated blood pressure (get a blood pressure cuff and monitor it if you are concerned—and follow up with your doctor
- lack of energy or loss of motivation
- susceptibility to frequent colds or other infections, or aggravation of existing allergies or asthma
- rapid heartbeat; rapid breathing; sweating
- frequent headaches
- loss of appetite; overeating
- difficulty digesting food, diarrhea or constipation, stomach distress
- sexual dysfunction or loss of interest in sex
- frightening dreams that wake you up; sleeplessness
- impatient or short-tempered with others; withdrawn from social interactions; difficulty working or playing with others
- jumpiness or reactiveness
- inability to concentrate; distractedness (drifting off at meetings or during conversations with friends); constant worry or going over and over arguments and inequities in your mind
- missing or forgetting deadlines (such as paying bills or missing appointments)
- disorientation (forgetting directions to a familiar place), and
- use of drugs or intoxicants (including prescription drugs) to help you cope.

WARNING

If you find that you are out of control, or that you have serious thoughts about harming others or yourself, contact a mental health professional immediately.

Stress is not just a mental phenomenon—it involves your entire body and mind. It begins as a psychophysical response to a perceived threat that triggers the "fight-or-flight" response. That ancient instinct is the key mechanism by which your body and mind alert you to dangers and keep you from getting hurt by enabling you to defend yourself (fight), or to run (flight). Adrenal hormones are sent into the bloodstream, causing blood flow to increase to the big muscles such as legs, arms, and back. These same hormones change your brain and body chemistry, causing you to become hyper-alert and hyper-responsive.

All your major organs and organ systems undergo dramatic changes whenever the fight-or-flight response is activated. If stress is prolonged, as is usually the case in the process of separation and divorce, the immune system may also be affected—accounting for symptoms such as increased colds or difficulties with allergies.

In the wild, where the fight-or-flight response is a normal part of daily life, an animal will run or fight, completing the normal cycle of meeting stresses, and then return to a state of rest (unless it is eaten, injured, or subdued in other ways by its predator). In the civilized human world, we are more likely to override the fight-or-flight response as we attempt to seek more peaceful solutions. While this certainly has its advantages, it also means we hold much of our stress in our bodies. We stuff our emotions and allow our problems to mount up until the mere realization of all we have to handle itself becomes the tiger lurking in the jungle, threatening to devour us. We end up living our lives as if we are under attack 24/7—in other words, we live with chronic, prolonged anxiety. This sustained stress makes us susceptible to certain illnesses, including cardiovascular problems, gastrointestinal complaints, sexual dysfunction, irritable bladder, skin problems, aggravation of asthma or pulmonary disease, muscular problems such as "nervous tics," and even certain forms of baldness (alopecia areata).

While you may not be able to immediately get away from all the causes of stress in your life, you can learn to manage stress so that it doesn't threaten your health and ability to function well. This is a particularly good time to look at your diet, your exercise, your use of alcohol or other drugs, and your intake of caffeine, which can have a powerful impact on your nervous system.

10 Not-So-Hard-and-Fast Rules for Managing Stress

1. **FOCUS ON THINGS AS THEY ARE RIGHT NOW INSTEAD OF DWELLING ON THE PAST OR WORRYING ABOUT THE FUTURE.** Keep in mind that you cannot control either the past or the future. You can help to shape your future but only one small step at a time.

2. **TAKE ONE THING AT A TIME.** You may be facing what seems like an infinite number of challenges at the moment—and they can all seem to roll into one huge mass that threatens to run right over you. Instead of lumping everything together, take one thing at a time. As the philosopher says, every great journey begins with a single step.

3. **ASK FOR ADVICE INSTEAD OF COMPLAINING.** In talking with close friends and relatives, try not to burden them with your complaints and troubles. Instead, ask for their advice—and listen to it.

4. **ACT ON YOUR DECISIONS.** Whenever you have come to a decision about a challenge you can actually do something about, act on it now and do so resolutely. Taking positive action builds confidence in your ability to have an impact on your future.

5. **KEEP YOURSELF CONSTRUCTIVELY OCCUPIED.** Be with other people, especially in situations such as volunteer work or athletic events where you can enjoy immediate victories or accomplishments. Find activities where you feel useful and where there are fairly immediate personal rewards.

6. **PRACTICE FORGIVENESS.** Holding onto judgment and blame, even though you have been hurt, accomplishes nothing and only erodes your own mental health. Seek out books addressing anger and forgiveness, or seek spiritual guidance if you find yourself blaming others for your troubles.

7. **CONSCIOUSLY RELAX.** Seek ways to consciously relax for a period of at least 20 minutes each day. There are lots of ways to do this: learn to meditate or to use relaxation techniques that you can learn from a CD or book; take a walk in the woods; get a massage; sit and play or listen to music that you enjoy and find calming.

8. **ESTABLISH A DAILY ROUTINE AND STICK TO IT.** Create structure in your life, perhaps around meals or other routine events. It helps to foster a sense of security and continuity when life feels insecure and disjointed.

9. **UNWIND A FEW HOURS BEFORE YOU GO TO BED.** Put a curfew on any thoughts about your troubles or their solutions. Put them out of mind after 8 p.m. If you wake up in the middle of the night, listen to a relaxation tape or soothing music instead of dwelling on problems.

10. **YIELD TO CRISIS.** It's not always easy to recognize when we're in crisis. When you feel overwhelmed or unable to know where to even begin to solve your problems, don't cling to attitudes of "toughing it out." Rather, admit to being overwhelmed and seek help from a counselor, therapist, or physician to give you a hand over this rough spot. Many men resist the idea. But a little intervention can go a long way, and especially if you're not used to talking about your deep feelings, counseling can be a great way to learn emotional coping skills that will serve you for the rest of your life.

Recognizing and Managing Depression

Depression can also stalk people made vulnerable by the stress of a divorce. Depression is often characterized by a particular way of thinking: that the problem you're confronting is hopeless, that nothing can be done to make a bad situation better, that you are incapable of changing anything, and that the world holds no promise of anything pleasant for you. What results is a dulling of virtually all experience and a kind of circular thinking that keeps us trapped in our own hopelessness. In his book *Emotional Intelligence*, Daniel Goleman describes it this way: "Life is paralyzed; no new beginnings emerge. The very symptoms of depression bespeak of a life on hold."

Think about how many times during conflicts with your ex as part of your divorce, you've had the temptation to either lash out physically (fight) or storm out of the room and never return (flight). And think of the times you controlled your anger—hopefully—or told yourself, no, I won't run away from this. I've got to deal with this in a reasonable way. At such times, you exerted control over yourself and over normal fight-or-flight responses. Of course, you may have found yourself going over and over the same old problem in your mind, unable to let go of it and feeling hopeless about things getting better. Being trapped in unresolved problems this way describes very well the seeds of depression and, if prolonged, can lead to a pessimistic view of life.

Learn to recognize the signs of depression, because it can accompany long-term stress. As depression settles over your life, it can have a major effect on how you relate to your children, your work, your friends, and your ex-wife. Most people who are depressed report that they just feel like being alone. They feel pessimistic, even hopeless about life. The deeper the depression, the more we want to isolate ourselves.

Physical symptoms of depression can include:

- headaches
- backache
- muscle aches
- joint pain
- chest pain
- digestive problems
- severe fatigue
- sleeping disorders, and
- changes in your appetite in either direction.

Emotional symptoms tend to be very powerful when you are depressed. You might feel totally hopeless and very sad, even to the point where you think about harming yourself or at least wishing you were dead. (Contact a mental health professional immediately if you are seriously considering harming yourself.) Things that you normally enjoy can become unpleasant, or can just seem like too much trouble. Even things you could hardly imagine not wanting to do, like spending time with friends or having sex, seem boring or a bother. You might be irritable with others or anxious when you are alone.

The good news is that if the depression is stress-related there are ways to feel better pretty fast. The remedies can involve everything from stress management classes to medication. Sometimes just removing yourself from situations that depress you can reduce your stress and ultimately your depression. If you have a significant number of the physical and emotional symptoms described here, make an appointment with a counselor or therapist and talk to them about your feelings. Depression can be treated. Get yourself out of it, for your own sake and for your kids.

Choosing Your Problems

You can only handle so much at any given time. If you try to take on too much, something will give, and it could be your health or your family relationships. What is too much? That may be the $64,000 question. In the midst of divorce, even the most basic task can seem like too much. Divorce is already an overload, and the more choices you can make that lessen the burden, the better off you'll be.

Most men—in fact, most people—don't take the time to develop a big picture about what has to be done and then set up clear priorities for accomplishing goals. We tend to take care of whatever is most pressing or glaring in the moment. It's the squeaky-wheel-gets-the-grease principle of management. This can work when you know you will have the time, energy, and resources to knock off each task as it comes. However, divorces have a way of heaping on new tasks at an alarming rate, and if you follow the squeaky wheel system there's a good chance you're going to quickly get behind. Once you're behind, it's easy to feel like things are hopeless—and let any ideals you had about being collaborative in the divorce fly out the window. You simply can't find the emotional fortitude to collaborate when you're getting buried alive. You go into survival mode where nobody matters but yourself, not even your kids.

To avoid ending up there, step back for a look at the big picture. Then sit down and make up a list so that you can prioritize, dedicating the most energy to the things that will have the greatest positive impact in the long run. In case you don't even know exactly where to begin, here's a list of all the things you might be juggling at this time:

- work issues
- money issues
- quality time with the kids
- legal issues
- communication issues with your ex
- personal needs

- social time, and

- home maintenance.

Each of these categories can, and usually does, include a complex range of issues. For example, work concerns might include anything from looking for a new or better job to personal problems with someone else at work. Work issues might spill over into other categories as well. For example, Gene's work as a sales representative often required him to be out of town for two-week periods. This meant that scheduling time with his kids was a problem. Flying back for the weekend to be with them was expensive, and the extra travel was hard on Gene himself. He eventually worked out new schedules with his employer that minimized the number of weekends he'd be away, and he scheduled regular phone calls with the kids for those days he was on the road. This took time and effort and, at the beginning, seemed to Gene an overwhelming task.

To get started on your own priority list, you'll probably want to make the things on your list more specific than what's listed above—for example, on Gene's list it wouldn't say "work issues," but rather something like "talk to Bob about minimizing weekend travel," or "get phone cards for the kids," or both. After you've made your list, ask yourself what priority level each item is. If you have a friend to brainstorm with, that may help you sort things out. Here are questions you might ask yourself as you prioritize:

- **HOW URGENT IS IT TO ADDRESS THIS ISSUE RIGHT NOW?** Is it worthy of a significant investment of my time and resources?

- **WHO OR WHAT WILL BE AFFECTED IF I IGNORE THIS CATEGORY FOR NOW—WHAT WOULD HAPPEN IF I SIMPLY CROSSED IT OFF MY LIST?** Is this one of those things that might come back to bite me somewhere down the line if I don't do anything about it right now? Will putting it off have a negative effect on relationships that are important to me?

- **WHAT IS THE BIG PICTURE ON THIS ISSUE?** Am I missing anything?

These questions will help you figure out whether the item can be safely ignored for now, or whether it needs your attention right away or soon. Be creative when trying to solve your problems. For example, when Howard found he had to fully furnish his new apartment and had no money to do it, he invited his friends to a housewarming party and asked them to bring along any furnishings they wanted to get rid of. Overnight, he ended up with everything he needed to make his new home quite comfortable. Eclectic, sure, but it worked for him.

Ask each of these questions with an open mind. Try to push past any resistance you might feel to thinking about the issue, and try to hold your focus even when dealing with the issues that carry an emotional charge for you. The sooner you can set priorities for getting them done, the better you'll feel. Having a vague to-do list hovering around in your brain can be a terrible energy drain and source of anxiety. Shakespeare wrote, "There is nothing either good or bad, but thinking makes it so." If you have a plan and a timetable for getting things done, you can focus your thinking on constructive ways to complete your tasks. You'll soon discover that this kind of constructive thinking greatly reduces worry and tension.

As you become more comfortable with the items you're dealing with, assign each task to a track:

TRACK A: Things that need your immediate and ongoing attention, without which there will be unacceptable consequences.

WHAT TO DO: Give this track your full attention, starting right now—even if it is just jotting down how you will accomplish your first steps—and follow through on what you plan.

TRACK B: Things that need your attention eventually, but can wait for now.

What to do: Decide how long you can safely put off attending to the items on this track. You are not ignoring these tasks. You will make a plan for when and how you will be attending to them, even if it is at some time in the future. Mark your calendar so that you remember to return to them.

TRACK X: Write down things that you can safely ignore till hell freezes over, either with no major consequences or with consequences that you and others can live with.

WHAT TO DO: Cross out everything that you can honestly say belongs on this list, and forget about it.

You may want to break Track A into smaller bites as you go along. Maybe you'll discover that there are items within items that you will need to break out and place on this track or shift over onto Track B or even Track X.

Delegating a task to someone else is sometimes the best way to go. It may be a professional person, a close friend who is your advocate, or a trusted family member who is not afraid to step in and help—whether that means discussing something with your ex or helping you plan the menu for when your kids are with you. If it's the former, don't disregard the possibility that family members or friends who are close to you and to your ex-spouse might be good mediators between the two of you.

For example, Gene was concerned that if he missed his weekend visits with his kids when work took him out of town, his ex-wife might use this against him, claiming he was being an irresponsible dad. He'd already had several talks with her about this matter, and nothing positive had come of them. He realized that having another discussion with her was not going to be the best use of his time. After some inner debate, he decided to delegate the matter to his attorney. The attorney wrote a letter to the children's mom, telling her that while Gene's work had been taking him out of town, making it difficult to see his kids as often as he would like, it was not for lack of interest. He very much valued his relationships with his children. In this way, Gene and his attorney created a paper trail that showed, in writing, that he intended to be a responsible, caring parent. His attorney felt this was not altogether necessary, but doing it freed Gene of the stress he was feeling around negotiating the matter with his ex.

True Stories: Your Worst-Case Scenario May Not Be So Bad

As you go through your lists, play with worst-case scenarios. And I do mean play. Take it lightly. This might seem like it could be anxiety producing. But the point is to make decisions about what you can live with and what you can't. Here's a good example:

When Jared and Belinda were breaking up, their son, Thomas, was preparing to attend an excellent university. Because of the added expenses of the divorce and establishing separate households, paying his tuition would have put both parents way over budget. Jared considered putting the tuition on his charge card but when he calculated the cost he was overwhelmed. Jared's worst-case scenario was that Thomas would have to get a job close to home, live with his father for two years, and earn money for his tuition. When Jared presented this proposal to his son, Thomas was predictably upset. However, he went for it. He lived with his father, worked, and saved his money for a full year. By that time, Jared was able to pay off some debts and had received a large bonus at work. Between Thomas's own savings and Jared's improved finances, Thomas was able to go off to the university with everyone's sanity intact.

Chances are good that even your worst case scenarios may turn out much better than you might have imagined. In many cases, the solutions do involve lifestyle changes. They might even necessitate some difficult adjustments. Jared had planned for many years to have his son enjoy college without having to work. He had worked his way through college and vowed that his own son would never have to do that. With the divorce, Jared's vision of his own life had to change, and he had to break a promise he felt he'd made to his son. But everything did work out well in the end.

Some people faced with Jared's choices would have burdened themselves with second jobs, or further sacrifices of their own lifestyles or even their health. Jared knew that making heavier sacrifices could have resulted in his feeling resentful of his son, and he chose not to let that happen. In the end, father and son made some important new bonds, living together and learning more about each other. Their friendship actually deepened in the process, and Thomas came away from the experience with a better sense of his own capacity for earning money and helping to make his own dreams come true.

Letting Go of Your Problems

Once you've "chosen" your problems—that is, looked seriously at what your issues are and prioritized them, choosing the ones that are most important to deal with right away—my next suggestion might seem contradictory, because it is to let go of your problems. Letting go doesn't mean not acting or not taking responsibility for your life. It does mean not obsessing about your problems to the point that they dominate your life.

In Hugh Prather's *The Little Book of Letting Go* (Conari Press), he points out that, "Problems assault us to the degree that they preoccupy us. The key to release, rest, and inner freedom is not the elimination of all external difficulties. It is letting go of our pattern of reactions to those difficulties."

To illustrate what letting go really means, Hugh tells the story of having his writing time interrupted by the demands of his children. With his wife Gayle away shopping, he knew that it was his responsibility to cook the children's lunch and help his older son with homework. But as he left his study for the kitchen, he was annoyed that he had to stop his work. He'd been enjoying working on his new book and wanted to stick with it.

Halfway through attending to the kids' needs, he realized that he had made the task he was doing—fixing lunch and helping his son with homework—very unpleasant. And then he remembered what Gayle had said to him as she was rushing out the door to go shopping: "I think we should say in the book, 'Make your state of mind more important than what you are doing.'" Remembering this, he instantly knew she was right, and he knew that he was definitely not applying that principle to his own life at that moment. He realized that he didn't have to feel as he was feeling. After all, his feelings were his own. Wasn't it, after all, possible to be in a happy state of mind at that moment, even though he was unable to do what he really wanted to be doing? In that instant, he started tending to his state of mind, as Gayle had pointed out, and completed what he was doing with pleasure.

Granted, this is a simpler set of circumstances than what you're facing as you decide how to prioritize the things you need to do to complete your divorce and settle down to a more normal way of life. But the idea of making your state of mind more important than what you are doing applies to major things as well as minor ones. Realize that it is possible to let go of the dark feelings you may have around whatever you are doing. Prather points out that, "Ordinary people and ordinary events have surprisingly little effect on our happiness and peace until we add our highly personal interpretation to what just happened. Once we do this, we become victims of our own perceptions and believe that what we ourselves are doing to the world, the world is doing to us."

Letting go means observing the interpretations we bring to each moment in our lives. Divorce can be a great teacher of that. We might choose to go to an easier school, that's for certain, but if we pay attention to what's happening to us during the emotional upheaval of divorce, we might see how much fuel we bring to the hearth of our own misery. We fan the flames with our worry. We often put more energy into worrying about not doing something we need to do than we would put into actually doing it. Daniel Goleman, in *Emotional Intelligence* (Bantam), points out that worry is "a useful response gone awry— an overly zealous mental preparation for an anticipated threat." We humans can make good use of our capacity for mentally rehearsing everything from award-winning athletic events to making love to winning a lawsuit. But when mental rehearsal turns into worry and worry replaces action, it's time to shut off the drills and recitations and just get down to work.

If you hope to reduce the stress you are feeling, choosing to shift your energy toward getting things done is going to be critical. Remind yourself that your feelings are your feelings, and that, regardless of the external events that may seem to have created them, you are their author. Can you let them go? You can if you start shifting your perspective.

Think of this as a time to rebuild your life by making conscious choices and decisions. Look for activities in your community, or among your circle of friends, that will nurture you emotionally, spiritually, physically, and intellectually. Whatever you do along these lines will help to ease the stress you are experiencing. But broaden your perspectives even here, thinking of these new activities not only as addressing the problems of stress but of opening you to new possibilities and opportunities for meeting new people, expanding your knowledge, and having some fun and adventure.

Look around for programs that can do all this while combating any depressive moods you might be experiencing. Consider tai chi, yoga, walking, jogging, running, hiking, biking, swimming, weight training, aerobics, dancing, meditation, and relaxation training. Spend time alone in the country, on a mountain, hiking, biking, or swimming. Sometimes the best thing to do is to stay right where you are at home, curling up with a good book. Or consider taking art courses, learning to play a musical instrument, joining a book group, a soccer team, or a local drama group. Take up an activity that you've dreamed of doing but have not had the time for until now—maybe for you it's writing poetry or a book, learning to be a gourmet cook, or building wood furniture.

Find out what's available in your community. Look into community colleges or even take a course online. The world is filled with opportunities such as these. If your motivation is low or even nonexistent, have patience but also keep your eyes and ears open for that class or group that piques your interest or even your passion.

Don't Go It Alone

In a truly collaborative divorce, ex-partners do what they can to support one another, knowing that doing so ultimately benefits the kids. When you know that your ex is in need, look for ways to be helpful, even as you maintain clear boundaries that say, "While we ended our marriage, I care how you are doing and want you to be healthy and happy." This can be a definite challenge in the beginning, but you have only to turn that thought around to understand its benefit. Imagine your ex saying that same thing to you—how would it feel? Somewhere between the tension you are currently feeling and the moment (sometime in the future) when you can at last see yourself and your ex in a new light, as just two people doing their best to make their ways in the world, you can at least entertain the possibility of collaboration and start moving in that direction. You'll be making an important forward stride if you try to give and receive help from your ex, knowing you are both in need of support at this time.

At the same time, it's critical to remember the flight attendant's advice: *secure your own mask before helping others with theirs.* Sometimes, as we are doing our best to keep the collaborative process alive and well, we just run out of gas. At such times we need people around us to offer a helping hand. Keep in mind that just as you gain pleasure from helping others, so others can gain pleasure from helping you. You've got to let them know what you need, however, and you do that by simply asking.

When you ask for help, even if it's just for ten minutes of emotional support over the phone, make sure you are asking people who are open to helping you and who can offer the kind of support you need at that moment. At the same time, choose friends in whom you are genuinely interested, and take the time to inquire how they're doing. Friends want to know that we care about them, even when we are reaching out for their assistance.

MODEST PROPOSALS FOR SELF-CARE

- When you're feeling stuck or overwhelmed, reach out for help. Ask someone whose judgment you trust for suggestions or advice.

- When faced with issues that are so emotionally charged that you can't get even close to making a solid decision, seek out the assistance of a professional counselor.

- Put your energy into things that you can actually improve. Don't put time into lost causes, no matter how idealistic you may feel about them. If in the future you have the resources to return to those efforts, go back to them, this time with personal reserves that can put you in a good position to succeed.

- Look carefully at your personal lifestyle demands. Is it possible that you are living beyond your present means? If so, if your lifestyle hurting your emotional health? Your spiritual well-being? Your social or personal relationships? Examine the trade-offs carefully and make more informed choices.

You can try the suggestions in this chapter, or devise your own ideas, but whatever you do, make sure you take good care of yourself. It will pay off for you—and your kids—in the short run and the long term. ●

CHAPTER NINE

Birthdays and Holidays

Birthdays and holidays can be really tough, especially in the early days and especially if you spend them without your children. And even if you and your spouse have been through a difficult divorce and are still angry at each other, you can miss her as well. Why? Perhaps because each time you think of holidays and birthdays you spent together in better times, you are reminded of disappointments and of dreams you once shared. But take heart. As each year passes,

> *"The best portion of a good man's life is his little, nameless, unremembered acts of kindness and of love."*
> —WILLIAM WORDSWORTH

you and your family will become more comfortable with the new family structure and likely will create new rituals and ways to celebrate important events together.

Even when you're making the most basic interim parenting agreement after you and your wife separate, make sure your plan covers where the kids will spend birthdays and holidays and how you and your spouse will negotiate any changes. Without a plan, you leave a lot of room open for arguments with your ex—and disappointments for your kids.

True Stories: Learning That it's Not a Competition

Holidays and birthdays are the times we ordinarily set aside to relax, celebrate the lives of our loved ones, recharge our batteries, and let go of our everyday burdens. But holidays are difficult for divorced families, and parents can easily become self-centered and bummed out, and either consciously or unconsciously create a stressful atmosphere. Consider what happened to Vick:

"In that first year after the divorce, I took on every birthday and holiday like I was going to war. If the kids chose to be with Amy for their birthday, I took it as an attack on me, convinced she was doing something to alienate my children from me. Every unresolved feeling of hurt, abandonment, and confusion I still had over the breakup rose to the surface, and I saw fatherhood becoming a big competitive game, as if I had to keep score about who the kids liked best. And if I was feeling like the loser, I was sure it was Amy's fault.

My game was busted when I woke up one day, looked around me and had to accept the fact that my kids were avoiding me—and I frankly couldn't blame them. It's different now, mostly because I can't do that to my children anymore. Everyone loses in that situation—everyone— but especially the kids."

You may lose your spouse when you divorce, but you'll never lose the responsibility of being a strong, compassionate, and collaborative parent. You and your ex-spouse will always be your children's parents, so do everything you can to honor your children's relationship with their mother, regardless of how you might be feeling about her. If the kids express a strong desire to spend their holidays and birthdays with her, understand the importance of allowing them to do just that. This is when your collaborative parenting skills come into play. If there is a single message to bring to your children during holidays and birthdays, it is that things are okay, and that in spite of difficult times there's still space in our lives to celebrate. This is ultimately the best gift, though we may sometimes need to reach very deep within ourselves to find it.

Happy Birthday for All

What are the expectations around birthdays—for you, for your ex, and for your children? Making plans that work for the extended family isn't always easy, because there can be so many people involved in the arrangements.

If you don't have a comprehensive parenting plan in place, the general rule is that wherever the child happens to be staying when birthday time comes around is where the child will spend the birthday—which usually means the custodial parent gives the party. However, that's not always going to work out best for your kids. How it plays out depends in part on the ages of your kids.

Most younger children—say, five and under—live with their moms most of the time, though there are certainly a significant number of exceptions. If your young child is with Mom on the big day, and you want to attend the birthday party, ask in a respectful manner for an invitation. Volunteer to bring treats, pick up the cake, or help with other tasks and errands. It may be difficult to attend the party, especially the first one after your separation. But don't be sad, grumpy, or self-centered—this will only upset everyone, including the birthday child. If you feel comfortable being at the party only for a short time—maybe just long enough to deliver a present, a kiss to the birthday child, and a cheerful celebratory face—then that's what you should do. You may not want more than that, or your ex may not. Be sure to work it out in advance and let your child know what to expect, so that there won't be disappointment that you didn't stay longer.

Kids six and older generally gravitate toward where the fun is. If your children's best friends live in Mom's neighborhood, chances are pretty good that this is where they will want to be on their birthdays. Whatever your kids' ages, if they want to be with Mom on their birthday even though they're scheduled to be at your house, let them go and don't guilt-trip them about it. This kind of preference tends to switch back and forth—even when families are all together under a single roof and everyone is happy with each other. This is something most parents must come to terms with, regardless of whether there's been a divorce or not. The bottom line is this: Don't mess up your child's birthday. Do everything in your power to make it memorable and fun. This is no time for pouting.

If you're the party host, make certain you invite your child's mother and welcome her warmly to the party if at all possible. If there's still a good deal of strain between you and your ex, discuss the question of attendance with your ex. If you or your ex don't feel comfortable with her attending the party you are giving, or vice versa, then look at the possibility of separate parties. That might be easier on everyone.

True Stories: Sharing Birthdays Peacefully

"The first couple years after our divorce," Terry explained, "my ex and I couldn't stand to be in the same room together, so inviting each other to parties we had for Tessa was out of the question. Things are better now, but negotiating what to do at first was sheer misery. We finally agreed to have separate parties and sometimes there would even be a week or two between Tessa's mom's party and mine. But that didn't matter to Tessa. In fact, I'm sure she liked the idea of having her birthday celebrated twice. Things have softened up a lot between her mom and me since then, but Tessa still likes what we've come to call 'the two-party system.'"

Have a Happy Holiday

Like birthdays, holidays can be a source of stress and friction after a divorce, especially early on. Your final divorce settlement agreement will include a schedule of how you will share holidays, but in the meantime, just as with birthdays, you'll have to work it out as you go or prepare an interim parenting plan.

One way parents who celebrate Christmas sometimes share custody is to split the day, so that one parent has the kids for Christmas Eve and Christmas morning, and the other for Christmas afternoon and night. Another way is to alternate major holidays by year—again, for those who celebrate Christmas and might live too far apart to split the day, parents agree that Mom will have the kids for Christmas in even-numbered years and Dad in odd-numbered years. In the year that Dad doesn't have Christmas, he gets Thanksgiving—or maybe the Fourth of July, if that's a day on which you have a lot of family traditions, or whatever other holiday feels like a good trade.

Some families choose to spend holidays all together, even after the divorce. Usually this doesn't happen right away, but after a few years and some time for healing, some parents are able to put aside their differences and enjoy time spent together with their kids. Some even blend in new partners and children.

There are lots of other holidays that you need to deal with besides the major commercial ones—kids have days off school for Martin Luther King Jr. Day, Presidents' Day, and the days that the school is closed for whatever mysterious reasons the school district deems important. Then there's winter break, spring break, and summer vacation. There are two sides to these vacations—parents can argue about who "gets" the time with the kids, or on the other hand, there can be strife about who is "responsible" for taking care of the kids when they're not in school. It all depends on your perspective. Whether it feels like a burden or a prize, you and your ex will have to come to some decisions. Whatever you do, make sure it works for your children.

10 Tips for Keeping Birthdays and Holidays Sane and Happy

1. Be Flexible

"Grandma's coming to my party!" your young daughter excitedly tells you over the phone. This may be wonderful news for her, but not for you. Grandma, your ex's mother, can't stand the sight of you. For weeks, you've been planning a birthday party for your daughter at your house. After all, you have custody on that day. But now, with Grandma on the way, you know your party is going to get sandbagged. What are your choices? You can go along with it, or put up a fuss and insist on your "rights." From your daughter's voice you can tell that if she is going to enjoy her special day, Grandma needs to be included. And that means the party will be at your ex's. You're not going to spoil that. This is just the reality you have to work with.

You need to be willing to change your plans in response to the unexpected. It might feel like you're always the one required to be flexible. Well, that's what collaboration is about. And where your children are concerned, the best present you can give your child is to head off conflict about having fun on special days like birthdays and holidays. The collaborative rule for you in this situation is to adjust your agreements to fit your kid's needs.

But can you let your ex know that you're unhappy with the change of plans? Yes—in a calm voice, expressing your disappointment even as you acknowledge that plans change. By doing so, you provide a model for your ex, who might reciprocate one day.

2. Be Proactive and Plan Ahead

What if the shoe is on the other foot? Say your mother wants to come to town for your child's birthday. Give plenty of warning to everyone involved—maybe even the other Grandma, so she doesn't make conflicting plans. Plan ahead, ask for modifications in your agreements well in advance, and don't assume agreement until you get it. Always keep in mind that your new family arrangements require much more planning than when everyone was living under the same roof. Plan your holiday times well in advance, too. Two months' notice is not too much.

One way to avoid disappointment is to communicate early and often with the children and your ex. If it's hard to talk in person or by phone, use email or even send a snail mail letter. Give your children's mom plenty of time to think about your proposals and to respond. And keep in mind that pushiness usually produces more resistance than cooperation.

3. Be Kind and Generous

Especially during holidays, keep any bitterness you still feel over the divorce between you and your ex. If you can't say anything nice, just smile. Avoid putting the children in the awkward position of taking sides. Be as generous as you can with your kids about their relationships with their ex and the rest of the family. Encourage them to talk about the gifts they received and activities they engaged in with other family members they see over the holidays. Children often feel that if they have a good time with one parent, it will hurt the other's feeling. Let them know they can show happiness with both parents. Help your children shop for the other parent, sibling, grandparent, or stepparent. Children want to give gifts to the people in their lives just as adults do. Younger children have limited funds and often feel very awkward about buying gifts for the first few years after the divorce. Make it easier on them by offering to take them shopping for a present for Mom or their siblings.

4. Keep Your Word

Be particularly careful to follow through on whatever promises you make related to the holidays. It's extra important to keep promises to your kids around holiday times—the holidays are a big deal for kids. Try your best to hold your ex to her agreements, too. At the same time, don't be a complete control freak about it. If you make a federal case of keeping agreements no matter what, you'll eventually establish a reputation for being a jerk. And you'll be sorry when you need to ask your ex for some slack.

5. Include the Kids in Your Planning

Whenever it's reasonable, let your children help make the choices about when and where to celebrate the holidays, and with whom. But before asking their opinions, make it clear that all plans must be cleared with everybody involved. This will help teach your kids to be part of the collaboration between you and your ex. And if you end up not being with your children on a special day, let them help you plan a time when you can celebrate together.

The input into the planning can mitigate disappointment about being apart from you on a birthday or important holiday.

6. Create Two Holidays or Birthdays

Having two holiday or birthday celebrations for the children—one at your house, one at Mom's—is often a positive solution for extended families. Just make sure that the plans you make are collaborative and that they are made well in advance. This arrangement reinforces for the kids that they have two homes, and cements new family rituals and holiday customs. Don't worry about spoiling the children with too many celebrations (but see below for advice about spoiling them with too many gifts). More is better in this case, and they will be delighted with the double treat.

7. Avoid the Indulgence Trap

Okay, one more time. Many divorced parents, especially dads, are still reeling from their personal hurt and guilt over the divorce. They may be overwhelmed by these feelings and respond to the children's pain with too much money or too many gifts. Consider the following statement by Audre Lorde before falling into this trap: "I have no creative use for guilt, yours, or my own. Guilt is only another way of avoiding informed action, of buying time out of the pressing need to make clear choices, out of the approaching storm that can feed the earth as well as bend the trees."

8. Take Care of Yourself if You're Alone

Holiday time can trigger a resurgence of memories and melancholy feelings, especially if you are surrounded by couples and families. Your own birthday can trigger similar feelings, and these difficult feelings can be magnified if you are not with the children. As holidays or birthdays approach, if you know you're not going to get to see your kids, be sure to make special plans for the day. Avoid being alone if you can. Visit a friend or relative, plan a short getaway vacation with friends, or consider helping someone less fortunate. Reach out to those children and adults who do not have family to care about them. There are plenty of people in worse shape than you and your family. If you give of your time or other resources during difficult times, you'll clearly learn the truth of the old homily that sometimes it's better to give than to receive.

9. Build New Family Traditions

Divorced parents, especially dads, often make the mistake of trying to duplicate exactly the pre-divorce family traditions. But you'll be much happier and more satisfied if you create your own traditions for your new family.

True Stories: Proceed With Caution

Use caution. I have a friend who decided with his ex that in the spirit of being collaborative, they'd spend Christmas afternoon together, with the kids, just as in pre-divorce times. "How did it go?" I asked him a few days after the holiday. "Don't ask," he exclaimed. "It was miserable. Donna and I got into a major argument and things got nuts. I left the house two hours early with her screaming at me and both kids crying." Even if things go pretty well, as they sometimes can, being together like this can be misleading for the children who might harbor hopes for your reconciliation. Most children have fantasies about that, with or without any encouragement from the parents. After some years a blended holiday might work, but give your kids (and yourselves) some time to get used to the separation.

Let the children share in the planning, and they will enjoy the new rituals even more. When Alejandro was divorced, he was alone for the first holiday season, so decided to spend Christmas with his sister and her family in Guadalajara. While there he learned that his sister's family still celebrated the season just as his parents had done when he was a young child. When he returned to his home in the U.S., he determined that he would introduce his own children to those customs the following Christmas. Before this he had not even noticed that he had simply gone along with his ex-wife's plans for the holidays. There was nothing wrong with the way they'd done it, but now he had the opportunity to share something with his own children that he had enjoyed as a child, and build new family traditions

10. Nurture Your Blended Family at the Holidays

If you remarry or get into a committed relationship and your new partner has children, they will undoubtedly have their own ideas about how to celebrate holidays and birthdays. Discuss with your new partner ways that you can bring together the children from both sides of the family. Instead of imposing your own way of celebrating, get all the kids involved with planning what you'll do together and incorporating everyone's traditions, whether those involve special foods or other rituals. Ask questions and ask for suggestions from the kids. Engage them in creating rather than imposing a totally new tradition.

Birthdays and holidays are special times for you and your kids. Plan ahead, communicate clearly, and stay calm and flexible, and your extended family will have something to celebrate. ●

CHAPTER TEN

Kids, Friends, Dating, and Lovers

As a single father, your love life is going to be a lot different than it was in your bachelor days. Now that you've got kids and an ex-wife, the challenge is to integrate your romantic life with being an accountable and loving parent. Pursuing a collaborative relationship with your children's mother means that you will have to tread lightly for a while, remembering the emotional minefield suggested in the familiar quote: "Heaven has no rage like love to hatred turned, Nor hell a fury like a woman scorned." I would only add to this that fury of this kind is not the exclusive domain of the female sex. Be prepared to deal with your own reactions to your ex's new social life.

> *When seeking your partner, if your intuition is a virtuous one, you will find him or her. If not, you'll keep finding the wrong person.*
>
> —JOSEPH CAMPBELL

Even though you and your ex have made the decision to end your relationship, the emotional attachments that you've built over the years die hard. Some say it takes most couples between two and five years to dissolve the emotional bonds that once held them. Others claim it takes half the amount of time you were married. Of course there's no hard, fast rule, but there's no question that letting go and grieving is a lengthy process. You'll do well to err in favor of caution in romance, both for your own benefit and in the interest of maintaining the collaborative spirit.

If the letters I get from people reading my website are any indication, many men have a tendency to rush into new relationships and to let everyone in their lives know that they are back in the game. This is perhaps natural enough given that the trials and tribulations you've undergone during these past months have kept you tied in knots, and you may feel a need to relax, to heal, and to feel good about yourself as a potential lover and mate. But whether our motives are to heal our egos, satisfy our hormonal drives, or find a supportive and loving relationship, the potential fallout can be the same.

The Dating Game: Ready or Not?

As anyone who has ever been there will tell you, during the months immediately following your divorce you are a man on the rebound, meaning that you are bouncing back from the ending of your marriage. You are especially vulnerable, and you may badly need to feel desirable and lovable again. Or there may be a dark side to your rebounding, of seeking punishment for screwing up your marriage or looking for a way to get back at your ex for rejecting you. Depending on their intensity, these hidden motivations can be like magnets drawing you into relationships that you would normally avoid like the plague. "Rebound relationships" are the ones you enter into before you've fully grieved or healed from the loss of your marriage, and while they may have some short-term satisfactions, in the long run they will do you more harm than good.

If you feel compelled to go out and quickly find a new mate to provide another parent for your kids, resist this urge. Your kids are better off with you alone than with your transitional or rebound romantic interest. The nature of rebound romances is that they don't last. What will it mean to your children if they become attached to your new friend, only to experience another separation?

If you're still feeling pretty churned up emotionally, it is better to concentrate on your inner needs and on building a solid and healthy relationship with your kids than to plunge headlong into a new relationship. If you are constantly distracted by your feelings about the divorce— mourning the loss or celebrating it, caught up with anger, feeling betrayed or just plain disappointed—join a divorce group or find a good counselor or coach to work with. Reflect on conflicts you've had in past relationships and try to learn what it was in you that got you stuck. As the saying goes, those who do not learn from history are destined to repeat it. Give yourself plenty of time to come to terms with your past.

DATING BEFORE YOUR DIVORCE IS FINAL

You have to decide for yourself whether you're ready to date in the first place, but deciding whether to abstain from dating until after your divorce is a strategic question. Having romantic encounters before your divorce is finalized can be risky from a legal perspective, depending on where you live as well as the conflict level of your divorce. In some states, having a relationship with someone else is considered adultery as long as you are married, even if you're separated from your spouse. Some judges might not care, but others might restrict custody or visitation if they disapprove of your behavior. Even in states where dating during divorce isn't legally considered adultery, a judge might believe that it shows that you don't care enough about your kids, and factor that in to custody and visitation decisions. So don't take the issue lightly. Find out how the courts in your state view the matter.

The other issue, of course, is what effect your dating will have on your spouse, and whether it will make it more difficult to settle the divorce. Some of the stories in this chapter are about just that.

In general, the longer you've been separated, the lower the risks of dating. And once your divorce is final and issues of property and support have been decided, the world is your oyster—as long as you and your family are emotionally ready. Potential legal consequences aside, your priorities should be staying centered around maintaining the collaborative spirit in your relationship with your spouse, and protecting the well-being of your kids.

True Stories: Timing Is Everything

Kent and Belinda had been separated for three months when Kent began dating Dory, a woman he met at a conference. As a manufacturer's representative, Dory traveled a lot, and one weekend when Kent had his two children with him, Dory phoned to say she'd be in town. Kent made a date to meet her at the natural history museum with his kids. This was a place the children usually enjoyed, so Kent thought it would be an easy and relaxed way to get together. Besides, Dory had said she'd love to meet his children, and this would be a good way for all of this to happen.

Toni, who was seven years old at the time, blew a fuse when she met Dory. Apparently intuiting what was going on between her father and this stranger, Toni told her dad's new friend, "You're not my mommy. Go away." What followed was a major temper tantrum. When Kent finally got his daughter calmed down, she went into a funk and demanded to be taken home to her mom's.

Of course, the whole story came out as soon as Belinda asked her daughter what was wrong. And then it was Belinda's turn to blow a fuse. At the time, Kent and Belinda's attorneys were in the midst of precarious negotiations, and the following week Kent learned that the talks were off. It was weeks before proceedings got back on track, and this time negotiations were far less than friendly. On top of that, Dory ran. The last thing in the world she wanted was to get caught between feuding ex-spouses.

Well-meaning friends or relatives may try to push you into dating prematurely. Don't let them. Remember that this first post-divorce relationship is where a great deal of healing can take place. And no matter how eager you may be to jump into a new relationship, it's more important than ever to take stock of the collaborative values your new extended family will spur you to embrace.

Back in the Game

Your first job is to make sure that you are really ready to be back in the game. If you're pretty sure that you've worked through the worst of your grief about the divorce, aren't looking to punish your ex by getting involved with someone else, and are emotionally ready to start a new relationship, then it's time to move ahead.

When you're truly ready to date again, it can be great for you and your kids. Intimate adult companionship is an important part of successful parenting. It allows you time to be a grownup as well as a parent, to revitalize, to explore the many pleasures of being a truly collaborative helpmate and friend.

Whoever you date will, to one degree or another, become a member of your extended family, even if they never cross paths with your children, your ex, other family members, or close friends. Your new relationships can, and in most cases will, have a direct or indirect impact on your family simply because they will have an impact on you.

So here's some simple and important advice: choose wisely! Often we don't think too much about what attracts us to a person or what we really want in a relationship. What I've found in working with single fathers, however, is that being a dad tends to trigger some questions that might otherwise go unasked. No doubt it's because we recognize that the choices we make at this point in our lives aren't quite as simple as they once were. It may also be because we don't want to go through the trauma of divorce, or put our kids through it, again—so we intend to be very careful in choosing a new partner and potential mate. Here are some questions to ask yourself:

- **What specific physical, emotional, spiritual, and intellectual qualities do you find attractive in a person?** Are there certain personal motivations, religious beliefs, or political views that you insist upon?

- **What specific qualities will complement you, your children, and your lifestyle?** Are there activities and interests that you and your children enjoy that you'd like your companion to enjoy with you?

- **How important is it that this person relate well to your kids?** Is this a nurturing and patient person? How much or how little do they enjoy doing things for others?

- **What type of companionship are you seeking: Do you want a friend?** A date? An uncomplicated sex partner? Are you hoping to remarry and perhaps have another child? Or do you want to stay single but have an adult in your life with whom you can escape the pressures of family?

- **Are you willing to date another single parent?** If things work out well, this can lead to blending your families. Are you up for meeting the challenges of doing this?

Now that you are older and hopefully wiser in the ways of the world, it might seem that your chances for choosing and creating a successful love relationship are better than they were first time around. Sadly, statistics don't bear this out. Even more second marriages than first ones end in divorce. However, this is an opportunity to make use of what you've learned, particularly the collaborative strategies described in these pages. Remember that the goal of your collaboration is not just to make things easier for your kids and your ex, but also for your own life to be easier and more fulfilling.

As you start to date again, you may discover that you have doubts about your ability to maintain a long-term loving relationship. This is natural enough, and most people in your position experience something similar—

especially after a second or third divorce! If you really screwed things up in your marriage, a little soul-searching is a good thing, but try not to get stuck in your emotional doubt and pain. You are not the same person today that you were a year or even a month ago. Let the past be in the past. We all learn our most important lessons from our mistakes. Do not let your guilt, blame, or shame interfere with your doing it right this time around. Just take an honest look, do your inner work, and move on with a determination to put your lessons into practice.

If the fear of failure and rejection is so intense that it interferes with your ability to move on and find happiness, don't waste time. Get professional help. That's exactly what therapy, and occasionally medication, are for. Get over it and get on with it!

Dating and Your Ex

It's all too easy to tell ourselves that after we're divorced there are no longer any bonds with our ex-mates. Nothing could be farther from the truth. Even beyond the bond you share because of your children, old habits are hard to break, and caring about what your ex does or thinks is a habit of many years. Likewise, your ex continues to have feelings about you and the choices you make. Depending on how difficult your separation was, her reactions may be mild or extreme. She may not mind seeing you with another woman or hearing from the kids about the wonderful breakfast Daddy's new friend made for them, or she just might go ballistic.

I'm not, of course, advocating that you allow your fear of your ex-wife's reactions to run your life. We are not responsible for each other's emotions. But it is possible to take responsibility for keeping your relationship with your ex as collaborative as possible—and that won't happen if you are careless about how you bring a new person into your life.

If you can do it, the most mature approach would be to sit down with your ex and talk about dating. Is your ex going to be stung by the thought of you being with someone else? Would she like you to give her some warning that you are dating again? Would she prefer to not have to face that for a few more months? How comfortable is she with the kids knowing that you are dating? And what about you? Is seeing your ex with someone else going to set you off? Would it be a shock to you if you saw your ex's new lover doing a favor for her, such as repairing the plumbing in the house that had once been your home? Be as open yet diplomatic as you can be. You're probably going to be skating on thin ice here, and if that ice breaks, you're truly going to learn a new meaning for the phrase deep freeze.

It's easy to slip into the trap of trying to take care of your ex's feelings or looking for ways to avoid an emotional blowout. And it can be a fine line between that and having consideration for her feelings. At some point, your ex is just going to have to deal with the reality that you are no longer her husband and that you have a life of your own—just as you're going to have to give up your feelings of possessiveness towards her. Treat this time following the divorce as a period when you stay focused on making the transition as smooth and constructive as possible—for you, for your kids, and for your ex. And this means taking her feelings into account, even while knowing that you can't change them.

Remember that freaking out your ex can undermine any collaborative foundations you've gone to so much trouble to develop. You may not be responsible for your ex's feelings, but if she flips because you've been careless about how you've handled the situation, you and your kids are going to get hit with the fallout. Maybe your ex has been totally reasonable throughout the separation and divorce—but the day she comes by to pick up the kids and finds you and your lady having breakfast in your bathrobes, you might be in for some surprises.

True Stories: Timing Is Everything, Volume 2

Vicki and Lyle had been divorced for six months when he began dating Katherine, a woman he'd known since high school. One Friday night after dinner and dancing, Katherine stayed the night, and Lyle totally forgot that Vicki was dropping the kids off at seven a.m. on her way to work.

"When the doorbell rang, I was sound asleep," Lyle told me. "But the instant I heard it I was out of bed like a lightning bolt."

Lyle and Vicki had been pretty friendly up until then. Whenever she dropped off the kids, they usually had coffee and spent some time talking while the kids settled into being with Dad for the day or the weekend. They had agreed it would be good for the kids to see that Mom and Dad were still friends.

"That morning was sheer hell," Lyle continued. "The living room was a mess—it was obvious someone was there. There was no hiding it. I'll never forget the look on Vicki's face. Katherine heard Vicki crying and stayed in the bedroom until everything settled down and Vicki left. But the damage was already done. I apologized all over the place, tried to tell Vicki that I never stopped to think that she'd still be jealous—all that kind of thing. But everything I tried to tell her was only digging my own grave."

Vicki gathered the kids around her and bolted from Lyle's apartment like it was a house of horrors, which it no doubt was for her. For weeks she made it difficult for Lyle to see the children. He had worked hard to build a collaborative relationship with his ex, and it had all been destroyed in that single morning. To get things back on track, Lyle offered to have a couple of sessions with Vicki and their old marriage counselor. Vicki agreed. In counseling, Vicki was able to acknowledge that she had been shocked when she discovered her own jealousy, and she took responsibility for her own feelings. At the same time, she asked for Lyle's promise that he would be a little more considerate of her feelings in the future—at least for a year or so.

Introducing Your New Love to the Kids

When parents start dating after a divorce, their children often aren't ecstatic about it. They may see this new person in your life as competition for your affection. If they have fantasies about you and their mother getting back together, they may attempt to protect that fantasy by ignoring or being hostile toward your friend. Your dating might also reawaken the fears of abandonment that they may have experienced when you and their mom first split up and you were no longer in their lives on an everyday basis. As one father put it, "My kids were just sure that anyone I even shook hands with was going to steal me away from them."

And as Kent related in his men's group, "Ah, the kids! All I can say is that hope springs eternal where they're concerned. Three years after the divorce and over a year into my new relationship with Gail, my kids are still asking when I'm coming home. Their mom and I are on pretty friendly terms, and my shrink tells me that, for better or for worse, this feeds the kids' hope that their mom and I will get back together. My oldest daughter, Tessa, tells me, 'Dad, you and Mom get along so good, I don't see why you can't get back together.' How do you explain stuff like that to a 12-year-old girl? I just tell her that her mom and I decided that we are better as friends than we were as husband and wife and that's the way we've chosen to live our lives. Does Tessa buy it? Hell, I think she probably spends half her life turning it around in her mind, trying to understand what she can do to get her mom and me back together."

True Stories: A New Friend

When Jenny was four, her parents divorced. The very first time she came to visit her father, Jerold, at his new house, Jerold invited his friend Colleen over to have dinner with them. Colleen was a nursery school teacher and dearly loved her work with children, so she was looking forward to meeting Jenny. Before Colleen got there, Jerold prepared Jenny's favorite dinner, macaroni and cheese, and set three places at the table. When the doorbell rang, announcing Colleen's arrival, Jenny dashed to the door and opened it just wide enough to peek at the young woman standing on the porch. Then Jerold heard Jenny say, in a very loud voice, "Go away. I don't want another Mommy." She slammed the door in Colleen's face and ran into her bedroom.

After opening the door to let Colleen in, Jerold apologized for his daughter's behavior. "It's fine," Colleen told him. "I know exactly what she's going through."

Colleen knocked gently on Jenny's door and asked to come in. After several minutes of coaxing, Jenny opened the door a crack and peered out. Colleen assured her that nobody would ever replace her Mom but maybe Colleen could be a friend. Jenny wasn't convinced. It would take several months for her and Colleen to make friends. In the meantime, Colleen was the one who set the boundaries, making certain that Jenny and her dad were given time for each other. Colleen minimized the length of her visits when father and daughter were together, letting Jenny know that she wouldn't have to compete with Colleen for Jerold's attention.

At the opposite end of the scale, some older kids are going to take the position that your having a friend means that you're becoming a self-centered parent, more interested in dating than with healing conflicts in the family.

Because of your children's lingering hope for a reconciliation, a new romantic partner for either parent is going to put them through some changes. It could anger the kids and they might feel betrayed by the dating parent, worried that this new person might take you away from them and this could mean even more abandonment for them. What can you do about your children's anger, fear, or resentment? Family experts say to just keep reassuring your kids that you love them and that you will always and always be their dad.

Be Cautious

Don't be too casual about bringing your new friend into your extended family. Until you are pretty sure the relationship is going somewhere, don't make your new friend a part of the home scene. For one thing, your kids might not be ready for you to begin dating at the same time that you find yourself ready. But more important, you don't want to risk the kids getting attached to a new partner and then have the relationship not work out. Sometimes when children, especially younger ones, see that you are relating to this new friend in an especially affectionate way, they might begin to allow themselves to open up emotionally and become involved with your new friend as well. It would be a shame if they made this connection and then you (or your new girlfriend) broke it off.

It happens, there's no doubt about it. It is just part of life. If you're on top of things as a parent, you'll then have to spend some time allowing your child to mourn that loss by simply sympathizing with them. As one man put it, "My daughter was heartbroken when Yvonne and I split up. I told her that I was going to miss Yvonne, too, but that together we (his daughter and he) would get through it."

Definitely don't bring your new friend home or introduce her to your kids until after you feel that your new relationship is a significant one. You'll know by the amount of time you are spending with her or because you begin talking about your future together. You'll know because of the way you get along, how well you can work out conflicts when they arise. And certainly you'll know it if you are talking about getting married or living together.

THE OVERNIGHT DILEMMA

It's wise to avoid having your new woman friend stay overnight until you've been with her for a while—maybe three or four months. At least wait until the kids are comfortable with your new partner, and until you believe this is going to be a long-term relationship. Otherwise have your overnights someplace other than in your home. Plan a weekend get-away, stay at your partner's house, or at your house when the kids are with their mother. It's cool to have your partner stay quite late, but you don't want your children asking, "Who's that person in your bed?"

Okay, so you're pretty sure you've found the new love of your life. She seems like she might just be the one—and you want to share your excitement and happiness with the kids. This is a big event for the kids. How should you handle it?

There are no hard and fast rules for what to do or say. In the end, it's not what you say so much as how you act toward your friend, the kids, and your former spouse during this time. The best advice I can offer is to stay on track with what you've learned about the collaborative way of life. Be understanding and patient. Make it clear to your kids that you have friends just as they have friends. (Sometimes, you even have *sleepovers* with a friend!) Make it clear to them that even though your friend sometimes spends a lot of time with you, she is not going to replace them in your heart, and she is never going to replace their mom. Tell them their mom will always be their mom and nothing will ever change that. Not now or ever.

Reassuring them might take far longer then you would like, and you might have to explain all this a hundred times, but suck it up and be patient. Eventually your children will get it—especially if you walk your talk and continue spending quality time with them that isn't diminished because of your new relationship.

When you're caught up in the pleasure and excitement of a new romance, you run the risk of unconsciously neglecting your children emotionally or even physically. It's important to keep spending quality time alone with your children and to maintain that time as a top priority as this new relationship takes shape. If you're the noncustodial parent or if your children are with you for only brief periods of time, make sure that when they're with you, the kids get your time. For example, your friend could come over for dinner one night, and perhaps the next time come back to visit after the kids are asleep. Or, better yet, you can wait until the kids go back to your ex's place and then enjoy time with your friend.

Children, even young ones, can be remarkably resilient, but it's important to keep in mind that there are limits to what they should be expected to handle. Is your child having difficulty with your having this *other* relationship? Whatever you do, don't avoid their questions or protests, and don't pull rank on them to end the fuss. Those tactics will only create further tension, and they are anything but collaborative. This is a time to call up all your resources for being understanding and compassionate towards your children, knowing these introductions can really bring up some fear and pain for them—and maybe for you. Let your kids know that you realize how uncomfortable this makes them, how hard it is for them to think about bringing a new person into their life. Assure them that you will always be there for them, and you will always love them. Repeat this frequently, and repeat the reassurance that their mom will always be their mom. If I seem to be repeating myself here, it's because I can't emphasize strongly enough that kids need to hear the reassurance over and over.

A child who is easygoing and who seems to openly accept your friend may or may not be showing what's going on inside. Be careful, thoughtful, and considerate, as tender young souls want desperately for you to understand what they may not yet understand about themselves.

True Stories: Still Waters Run Deep

When my friend Ginger's ex-husband got remarried, they all thought everything was fine with four-year old Grace. "Anything but!" Ginger told me. "Tom wanted her to be their flower girl. I was okay with that and thought Grace was, too. A week before the wedding, Gracey had a meltdown. I didn't see it coming. She broke out in a rash and we thought she had the measles. The doctor said it was allergies but we never discovered to what. When we got home from the doctor, Grace climbed into my lap and wept uncontrollably. I just held her and let her cry. When she finally stopped she asked me, 'If Daddy marries Kate, where will you go, Mommy?' And that's when I got it. Poor little Grace! She thought if Tom married, Kate would become her mother and I'd disappear. I cry any time I think of what a big load she was carrying. She actually thought Tom would send me away."

Grace had always been an easygoing if not reticent child who rarely let others know her feelings. Everyone assumed that she was just a very flexible and laid-back kid. In fact, the incident involving Tom's wedding revealed to everyone that she was extremely sensitive and somewhat withdrawn into her own fantasies of how things worked in the world. Whenever potentially emotional issues arose after that, Ginger, Tom and Kate always took extra time to give Grace plenty of opportunity to express herself.

Talking with Older Kids

You can safely assume that your teenaged children will have a pretty sophisticated view of what's going on between you and your friend. So you're probably going to be okay talking with them openly. But don't assume too much. It's not just a question of how honest you can be with your teenagers; it's more a question of how much detail you should go into. Your teenager isn't your best friend, and doesn't need to know what goes on between you and your new partner except in the most general terms. Serena's mother Alee told her 16-year-old daughter about her father's new girlfriend. Serena immediately telephoned her father, Wayne. "I can't believe you didn't tell me first," Serena said. "Dad, I thought I was your closest confidante!"

Somewhat taken aback, but realizing his daughter was teasing him, Wayne came back with, "I was waiting for the right moment."

"Oh, get off it," Serena said. "You just chickened out, didn't you? You told Mom so she'd tell me." While this wasn't exactly factual, it was true that he'd broached the subject first with Serena's mother, who had remarried the previous year, and asked her advice about how Serena should be told. When Alee volunteered to discuss it with Serena, he didn't protest.

"So, Pops," Serena said in a mocking tone. "Are you getting it *on* with her?"

Wayne, of course, was flabbergasted. "Hey," he said. "That's none of your business."

"Well, that probably means you are, doesn't it?" Serena said. "You're really embarrassed, aren't you?"

Wayne admitted he was. Only then did his daughter let up. "I'm sorry, Dad, I just had to give you a bad time. I'm actually really happy for you. I really am." As Wayne would tell me later, "You never know quite what to expect from teenagers these days!"

Don't assume, however, that your teen will be as open and cheeky as Serena. For a million different reasons, they could be quite uncomfortable with your having a serious love interest, and especially with the prospect of your remarrying. Take it one step at a time. Carefully listen to your son or daughter's responses—what they say, what their facial expressions tell you, and what their body language says. Teenage boys are usually practiced in deadpan responses, betraying little or no emotion. And the more emotional the situation, the flatter the deadpan expression. If you're simply getting nothing back—no words, no feedback of any kind—don't push it. Just put out a bit of information today, a bit more a few days from now, and so on. Chances are excellent that as they sit with this information they will get curious about it and start asking questions. Be patient.

If you have two or more older children, talk with each one individually and tell them how you feel about this person. Give out only enough information at any one time to test the waters. Be open. Tread lightly. Watch for the surfacing of different emotions. Be aware and sensitive to their responses, but don't let them run your life. You have every right to be happy, especially to have a happy, constructive, and loving relationship. In the long run, your fulfillment in this relationship can provide a positive model for them. Especially if your divorce has been contentious, seeing a healthy and happy relationship can be a wonderful antidote.

You're the Boss of You

Both your children and your new partner are important to you, but don't let any of them completely run your life. You decide how to handle your choices, opportunities, and responsibilities. If your children don't like the person you date, or a person you date does not like your children, this will obviously not be a very workable way to live. Maybe they're jealous of one another, each wanting all of your attention and love. Maybe they're just not ready, and you need to slow down in terms of contact between the kids and your new partner for a while, and see if that eases things up. If you're feeling hassled or tense over this issue, you may want to talk with a professional counselor to help you sort through what is happening.

One of the big challenges in any relationship has to do with being clear about your own needs and wishes. We all have to make some accommodations to the others we share our lives with. This can range from not leaving your dirty socks on the living room floor to not dating other people. But we all have core values and needs that are so important to us that giving them up would mean abandoning ourselves for the sake of someone else's comfort.

What kinds of accommodations are going too far? What is non-negotiable? Your love for your children, for one thing. If your friend tells you that you must make a choice between her and your kids, kiss her goodbye and don't look back.

True Stories: Parenting 101—Not

Brock had been married for eight years and had two children, Gabby and Trish, when he and his wife split up. Two years later Brock started dating Libby, a woman he'd met through a cousin of his. She was a schoolteacher and at first seemed to like spending time with Gabby and Trish. The only trouble was that she took is upon herself to give Brock ongoing parenting lessons, which started the moment she entered the house and stopped only when she left.

"It wasn't that she didn't have good ideas," Brock said. "The problem was that she'd step in when I was disciplining one of the kids and tell me I was doing it all wrong. Then she'd demonstrate the right way—well, her right way. No argument that she knew some good tactics—but pretty soon the kids were avoiding her like the plague. They didn't like what she was doing any better than I did. I tried to follow some of the things she told me to do and often they didn't work for me. They worked for her; they didn't work for me.

"Then the kids started rebelling. They wouldn't pay attention to either of us, and I was losing all confidence in my fathering skills, such as they were. I confronted Libby with the problem and she was adamant. She told me in no uncertain terms that she knew she was right and I was wrong because she was very successful in the classroom and if I wanted to keep doing things my way I was going to create a very dysfunctional family situation and she didn't want any part of that. Well, sadly, I suppose, we parted company the next day. I don't know if I'm being a dysfunctional parent or not but my kids are happy, pretty well-behaved, and doing well in school. And me? I'm still single but I have great friends and my life is pretty damn good. I'm not complaining."

While it's not always easy to walk that thin line between demanding respect for who you are and accommodating the people you love, it's an important line to be aware of. Depending on how you handle it, you'll give your children a model for either developing their own wholeness and inner strengths or becoming a slave to other's wishes and abandoning their greatest inner gifts.

When Your Ex Starts Dating

As fraught with difficulties as dating after divorce can be, at least you're making your own decisions about when and whom to date. But what about when the shoe is on the other foot? How are you going to feel about your ex's dating? It might be easier to say than to do: You can't control your former spouse's love life, but you can control your attitude toward her dating.

It is important to understand and accept the fact that you cannot choose whom or when your former partner dates. Even if you feel a great sense of relief about not being married to her anymore, you may be surprised to find waves of jealousy sweeping over you when you discover that she is intimately involved with another person. You may feel anger at being replaced, sadness at the realization that the marriage is truly over, or fear that your children will like the new person more than they like you. Or, you might feel happiness or relief that your ex is getting on with her life.

This is all normal. Long-standing relationships and feelings do not end or change the minute the judge signs the divorce decree. Be aware of these feelings. Share what you are feeling with a close friend. Do everything you can to take full responsibility for what you are feeling, and don't lay your feelings on your ex or your children.

And don't let those feelings come out in inappropriate ways that will undermine your efforts to stay cordial with your ex. Don't, for example, make remarks to your children about that Bozo your mother is dating, or to your ex such as, "I can't believe you're sleeping with that Neanderthal. It's so beneath you!" (Of course, all of you reading this book—just like me—are way too sophisticated and refined to even think things like this. Right? Sure we are.)

It's going to take some time to deal with these feelings and fears— particularly the first time you go over to pick up the kids and find your ex's new boyfriend helping your young son to get dressed. When that happens, take a deep breath, let it out slowly, and be friendly and polite, reminding yourself that the longer you hold onto old attachments to your ex, the longer it's going to take you to step fully into the new life you're creating for yourself and your kids.

Use every principle that you've learned about collaborative divorce and you'll get through this one, too. You can have it all—a great relationship with your kids, relative peace with your ex, and a fulfilling relationship with a new partner. Just be sure to take your time and be deliberate about creating the life you want. ●

CHAPTER ELEVEN

Taking a Chance on Love Again: Remarriage and Blending Families

Any successful marriage involves sharing our lives with someone, learning to be open, and being able to face difficult challenges together. But if feedback from men's groups and online sharing at my website is any indication, it is not widely understood that second marriages, especially where children are involved, have special challenges that first marriages don't have. These take a number of forms. You will have an ongoing relationship with your ex by virtue of the fact that she's the mother of your children and you must, at the very least, coordinate visitation rights. If you've established a cooperative and friendly relationship, you will have incorporated her into your extended family. While this makes things more comfortable for the kids, and possibly for you, it may complicate your relationship with your new wife or partner. Consider it from your new spouse's point of view; she is not just dealing with one new relationship, meaning you, she is also going to be dealing with your children and, to a lesser degree, your ex-wife.

> *A good marriage is one which allows for change and growth in the individuals and in the way they express their love.*
>
> —PEARL S. BUCK

The other big issue is blending your new partner into your existing, immediate family unit—the one that now consists of you and your kids. There's your new partner's relationship with your kids to work on, as well as your relationship with her kids, if she has them, and the kids' relationships with each other. And that's all on top of the primary relationship that you're entering into with your new partner.

Given the challenging realities of blended families, it's good that you've been developing collaborative skills. They will be invaluable assets in your new relationship, just as they have been in your continuing and ever-changing relationship with your ex. With those tools, you'll be prepared to handle the issues that are inevitably going to arise.

WHAT IS MARRIAGE ALL ABOUT?

Having a realistic picture of married life is just as important as having collaborative skills. You've had your hard-won lessons, of course, but I also like to refer people to *Reflections on the Art of Living: A Joseph Campbell Companion* (Harper), where Campbell reflects on the inner workings and universal aspects of marriage:

- "There are lots of joyful experiences in marriage that have nothing to do with total rapture, but these experiences absorb that energy system and make it possible for one to stay married and not think only about taking out the garbage. Anyone who gets married is going to have problems with the daily chores...But you can make wonderful ritual experiences out of things that have to be done, and life can ride beautifully on these events. I think it's the failure to accept the tangibilities of two people living together that make marriages break up.

- "There is a kind of breakup that takes place late in marriage. I know people who are well into their 50s, or they have been living together, they've brought up a family together, had a life together, and it goes to pot. The only thing that was holding them together was the children. This is the failure of what I call the alchemical marriage. They have had the biological marriage, but there has been no realization of the interlocking of the psyches and the mutual education that comes from acquiescence and relationship...Successful marriages are about leading innovative lives together, being open, not programmed. It's a free fall: how you handle each new thing as it comes along is the most important element.

- "What you see in marriage, then, is the identification with the other person as your responsibility, and as the one whom you love. Committing yourself to destiny is a life commitment. To lose your sense of responsibility to the person who has given you their commitment because something seemingly better comes along that enables you to think, 'I'd like to fly off in this direction and forget that which has been already committed'—this is not marriage. I don't think you're married unless the relationship to your spouse is the primary consideration in your life. It's got to be tops. In marriage you are not sacrificing yourself to the other person. You are sacrificing yourself to the relationship. The key to marriage is compassion, suffering with, feeling another's sorrow and joy as if it were your own."

Not only are you marrying her, her children, and her family, but you are also inheriting her former spouse and his family—and vice versa. You will need to work hard to protect your relationship from the doubling of family responsibilities that each of you are taking on. Think about ways to keep the romance alive while you navigate the challenges of blending your families.

Parenting in a Blended Family

Don't forget the children's challenges. If both you and your ex remarry, your kids will have two sets of parents and four (or more) sets of grandparents. This extended family inheritance, with all its attendant baggage, is going to take long-term, careful, and thoughtful integration and nurturing. Children can be tolerant or even supportive of their parents remarrying, but remember they've been through a lot: By the time you're ready for your next marriage, it might be a child's fourth family unit. The first was your marriage, the second the family unit of you and them in your house, the third the family unit with them and their mom in another house, and the fourth is the family unit being established with your new partner. Each time they had their own little worlds pretty much worked out, and then had to make a major adjustment to the new way of life. Now, with a stepparent coming in, the whole thing is starting over again. Another set of complicated routines to get used to. And... oops...who are these new stepsiblings showing up in their lives?

Your kids learned to live within the confines and challenges of their past lifestyle. They knew what to expect. They knew how to make it more or less work for them. They've got quite a bit invested in that lifestyle, and giving it up isn't easy. They need time to let go of all their attachments to that old way of life. Once released—as it will be if you give it a chance—they can more freely step into the life you are offering them.

ASK AN EXPERT

 YOU MAY WANT TO GET SOME HELP IN THE BLENDING PROCESS. In the best of worlds, your kids form a healthy bond with their stepmother, and new friendships develop between her kids and yours. Does this best-case scenario happen automatically? Usually not. If you see conflicts developing, either between your kids and your new wife, or among the kids, first recognize that they are normal under the circumstances, and then accept the fact that if you're going to successfully blend your lives, you might need the help of a family counselor. If you get a head start on recognizing what to expect and how to handle early conflicts, you've got a good chance of making your expanded family work really well.

It's quite normal for kids to hold on to the hope that Mom and Dad will get back together and life will return to how it once was, even if that wasn't a particularly happy scene. In the midst of your own adjustment to these changes, don't lose touch with what the kids are going through. Pay attention to their grieving process, because most often they are not mature enough to explain why they are unhappy. Instead, their discontent usually shows up in negative actions and attitudes, particularly toward those they might view as interlopers in their lives—and that can mean the new love of your life.

Be ready for your kids and hers to act out as your two families begin to blend. It's not unusual and is commonly an effort to establish their position in the power structure of the new family. Try to allow a generous amount of time and lots of forgiveness so children will have an opportunity to feel at ease in the new extended family. Don't take mischievous behavior too seriously.

True Stories: A Slow Jelling

"For months after our two families came together," Jonathan told me, "Willa's six-year old daughter Leela clung to her mom like glue. My daughters, who were ten and twelve at the time, certainly reached out to Leela but without much luck. Slowly, what came out was Leela's fear of losing her mom. Seeing her mother find what she called 'a new Daddy' was bad enough for her. Seeing that this new Daddy came with two new females was an added threat in her mind. I didn't understand it, and neither did Willa.

As we just dealt with it, what came out was that when Leela's father had an affair, he rejected both Willa and Leela—and her father's lover had actually treated this little girl with uncensored hostility. Leela somehow saw my daughters as being like her father's lover, and was afraid of being rejected all over again. In time, she gained confidence in all of us and, as far as I can tell, her wounds are healed."

You and your new partner each need to be the ones guiding your own children, and you want to all end up at the same destination, with values that are respectful of every family member. If the job seems too big for you, or you feel that there is little chance of successfully bringing your new partner into your family system, you may have to face the fact that this new relationship just might not work out.

WHAT IS A STEPPARENT?

When you remarry, your new spouse becomes a stepparent to your kids. If she has kids, you become a stepparent to them as well. A stepparent is a legal term meaning the spouse of a legal parent who is not also a legal parent. Your kids and your spouse's kids probably already have two legal parents. Just being a stepparent does not give you any rights with regard to your partner's kids—for example, you can't give them your name without a court order granting permission.

In order to be a legal parent, you would have to adopt them, and to do that you would have to have their other parent's consent. This sometimes happens, and if your spouse's former husband isn't at all involved with his kids and you want to adopt them, consider asking whether he would consent. But most of the time, kids in stepfamilies keep the same legal parents they had when they were born, and stepparents continue in a role where they are legally not related to the kids. This means that if you and your new spouse split up, you won't be entitled to share custody or have visitation with each other's kids. You also won't be responsible for paying child support for those kids.

Blended families should come with a warning: "Fragile: Handle with Care." At first everyone involved might have difficulty coping with the enormous changes that are thrust upon them as you all work out the logistics of the new living arrangements. Who gets which room? Who gets to choose the breakfast food? You and your new spouse might begin to feel like referees at the World Wrestling Federation. Getting through this requires negotiating skills, a great deal of patience, and a great deal of compassion for other people's wounds and broken hearts. Kids' emotions can range from fear and depression to anger and rage to non-cooperation, withdrawal, or conscious sabotage of the new family structure.

Possibly the most important thing you'll need is the ability to look beyond kids' acting out behaviors and understand how to help broken hearts mend. Holding family meetings, seeking occasional outside counsel, or joining a stepfamily support group are some options. Don't despair. Love, understanding, and acceptance of each others' feelings will likely heal these issues and build bonds that can last a lifetime. Be gentle and make plenty of room for the blending to take place.

You can eliminate a great amount of stress in the blending process, and head off many potential disasters, by making sure that each member of the new family unit feels loved and wanted. Husbands and wives set the standards of behavior and caring by showing a deep love and respect for one another. Their love spreads to embrace the children. Because it's way too easy for a quiet family member to fall between the cracks and feel unwanted, you must make conscious choices to love all members equally, even if they really bug you.

BUT THEY'RE NOT MY KIDS

One of the challenges you may face is that of living in a household with—and therefore parenting—kids who you really don't know well and who are not yours. You might feel guilty because you don't love your spouse's kids like you do your own, but remember that blending families takes time. You will naturally be more concerned with your own children, and you may be protective of them in the sibling wars that are likely to occur early on in your family transition. Don't beat up on yourself—all of this is completely predictable. At the beginning, allow your partner to parent her own kids more than you do, and assert your right to do the same with your kids. Over time, you can gradually ease into sharing the parenting more.

Blended families take time to truly blend. Realistic expectations between stepparents and children must include a gradual period of getting to know each other. One of the most common pitfalls that stepfamilies can fall into is the expectation that "we are one big happy family" from day one. This kind of idealization is often a setup for failure and disappointment. Instead, family members need to start from a place of simply respecting one another, and let relationships build on their own merit, without pressure to immediately become a fantasy family.

One father tells of his own struggles to give up what he termed his "peaceable kingdom" fantasy: "Natalie really didn't get to know my 12-year-old son Eric until after we were married. I had this idea that she and he would just naturally be friends, would love each other as much as I loved each of them. It wasn't to be. She and Eric are at loggerheads half the time. It got so bad, Natalie threatened to leave. That's when we all sat down together and set some ground rules. I made it clear to Eric that Natalie was my wife and I wanted him to treat her with respect. I also told him, in front of Natalie, that I loved him very much and that if he had difficulties with Natalie the three of us could sit down and work things out. This seemed to send a message to both of them not only that I loved them but that I was willing to help them work out any disagreements they had between them. While Eric never fully accepted Natalie, he did in time begin to treat her respectfully. And Natalie comes to me when Eric pushes her buttons. It's a bit disillusioning to see the truth that we're not one big happy family, but at least there's relative peace in the family most of the time now."

You'll probably discover that the greatest challenge of remarrying comes about because each family member is entering an already established system set up by the other family. Both systems evolved through the existence of the family started with the previous spouse, and then evolved as the kids came along and new challenges were encountered. What kind of guidance will the children need, and who will provide that guidance? In short, how will you and your new wife integrate your family systems? The odds are that the children are going to test each of you to see who is worthy of membership in this system, and they'll do it in a very personal and sometimes confrontational way. Your responsibility as parents is to work together to build a sense of security, safety, and happiness for all concerned.

The Discipline Issue

It's vital in any marriage for the parents to present a united front when disciplining the children. This cannot be emphasized enough. Resolving tough parenting issues through heartfelt sharing, understanding, and backing each other up builds collaboration and intimacy between the parents while building trust with the children. Remember to be patient with your desire for quick positive change. Even when things are toughest, remind yourself that intimate relationships develop gradually and are built on genuine affection, understanding, and confidence.

Discipline can be particularly problematic in a blended family because it's difficult to be very effective before your partner's children really know and have bonded with you—you can't just step in and supply parenting wisdom before you've developed at least some level of mutual trust and affection. Until then, you and your partner need to have agreements about goals and expectations, but discipline needs to be the responsibility of the biological parent. You and your new partner may disagree, so take the time to sit down and discuss rules and discipline on a regular basis. Don't push it with her kids. And if you are expecting everything to be done your way, forget it. The most successful blended families are the result of a lot of compromise and a lot of skillful communication.

If your new spouse's children are teenagers, it might never happen—the kids may always see you as an outsider. Don't sweat it. It is not realistic to believe that your parental authority will develop in the same manner with a teenager as with a young child. Respect the teen's boundaries and what has come before, and if necessary, seek the help of a counselor to as you build your new family system.

All the changes you and your new partner are creating in your lives take time to bring to fruition. Don't get down on yourself or any of your other family members if what you envision doesn't happen all at once. Creating a healthy family is a true collaborative effort, one that works best when you include the youngest as well as the oldest in major decisions. All the collaborative experience you accumulated while dissolving your previous relationship now comes full circle, for these are life skills that apply to all human challenges, now carrying you toward one of life's greatest rewards: the creation of a relationship that will endure the test of time.

Sibling Rivalries

Feuds between siblings can form patterns of behavior that are repeated again and again throughout a person's life. Classic sibling rivalry occurs when a child feels it's necessary to compete with a brother or sister for a parent's attention. This can be magnified in a blended family, because children may feel that there are just too many people to compete with. Rivalries develop not just because the child feels there is too much competition, but because one or both parents simply haven't been emotionally available. Kids shouldn't be expected to have great insights about that; after all, most adults don't always see it. Rest assured, however, that when Dad's not available emotionally, each child will be sure that he or she is the only one not getting love and attention. And what most kids will experience is a sense of deprivation and a feeling that all the love is being given away to someone else. If you are blending families with kids on both sides, it's easy for each child to blame this on a sibling or stepsibling.

Children from both sides may feel threatened by the newcomers, feeling that these "strangers" coming into their lives are going to take something away from them. If you have not been able to give your kids as much attention as they might have wanted or needed during the separation, they are going to feel doubly threatened.

AND BABY MAKES…?

One of the great challenges for a youngster, particularly one who's been an only child for a number of years, is having a new baby come into the house. The insecurity and jealousy that bubbles up at such a time is completely natural, and you can't really stop it from happening. However, there are a few tips to help you keep it from getting out of balance. Cut the kids a little slack, and assure them as much as they need. In many cases, getting an older child to participate in getting ready for the baby can help them feel that they are important and are contributing to this major life event.

As your new wife begins to show her pregnancy, get some books that are age-appropriate for the older child that help to explain what's going as the baby grows in its mother's body. (Yes, this is for boys, too!) Most children will become increasingly curious and interested in the birth. Have them help you fix up the baby's room. Ask them to help you pick out equipment you'll need. The more involved the child is, the better, and the less rivalry you'll be likely to see.

Make Space for Mourning, and Change Will Happen

By joining up with a new life partner, you may feel very happy to be bringing benefits into your children's lives—greater stability, a more caring and loving environment, or financial advantages. But you may still run into a lot of resistance. This may seem to you like the basest ingratitude—after all, why would anyone not be receptive and open to great improvements in their lives? The answer is found in a simple truth: Change is difficult.

Your children need space to mourn what they are leaving behind as they transition into this new way of life that has been thrust on them. You may look at what they are leaving and what they are gaining and think to yourself, "How could they possibly mourn what they are putting behind them? What they are gaining is so much more!"

But the kids may see any kind of change as frightening, especially if the changes related to the divorce were difficult. For example, maybe after your divorce two of your kids had to share a room, or move to an area away from their friends. Your own inner life might be improving as a result of getting a divorce. But the kids are only looking at the fact that, "Now I've got to share a room with my dumb sister." Or, "We're moving away and I'll never see my friend Timmy again, never in my whole life." Very definitely, you will be asking your children to make sacrifices, and many children can only see themselves as victims of your choices. This may make it hard for them to see that the future you're making with your new partner will hold many positive things for them—maybe even including a return to having their own room.

Through giving the children the license to mourn what they are leaving, you'll free them to move into the future that you and your new partner are creating. The children will eventually respond to the health and love present in your new relationship. Believe it or not, children really do want their parents to be happy.

Don't forget to mourn your own losses as you enter a new relationship. Parents also suffer loss, particularly if their children are not living with them.

New Family, New Rituals

It's important for new families to develop their own rituals, so don't come in with an agenda. You can't expect to just transplant your existing preferences into this brand-new situation. As your new family comes together, pay close attention to everyone's needs and expectations. This doesn't mean being blown about this way and that, like a leaf in the wind, as you try to go along with what everyone else wants. What it does mean is that you take time to learn about the needs of your new family and each of its members—what their likes and dislikes are, what their fears are, how flexible or inflexible they are in their dealings with you and other family members.

True Stories: New Routines

When Justin and Becky blended their two broods together, they were a seven-member family—the two adults, Becky's two kids, and Justin's three. "The first thing I discovered," Justin said, "was that Becky's kids rarely sat down to a meal together. The kids did tons of activities, and as a working mom, she'd prepared nutritious snacks that the kids could grab on their own—and everyone sort of grazed instead of having sit-down meals all together. Maybe it worked when there were just the three of them but it sure didn't work anymore. It took nearly a year to establish what I considered to be a normal evening meal and none of it was easy, but today we're all fairly satisfied with our meal routines."

As you are getting to know each other, be open in your communications. If the children are old enough to participate in family meetings and discussions, be sure to invite them to participate at whatever level is appropriate. This will help to give all members a sense of belonging to a new intimate group. Whatever rituals and customs you bring in, if appropriate, may become part of your new family culture—from the daily rituals of meals and shared activities, to the special ones connected with important holidays or other dates. New holiday rituals can be developed that are unique to the present constellation. For example, an Episcopalian woman marries a Jewish man and so Chanukah celebrations might be added to their usual Christmas events; the children learn new rituals and expand their philosophies for living. Other elements, such as specific kinds of goofing around and humor can also go a long way toward weaving a family together. Humor can foster a divine bonding experience, and finding ways to laugh together will go a long way towards establishing a sense of belonging to each other. Don't force these things—they will come with time, and one day you'll have a pleasurable moment of realizing that new habits and rituals are strengthening your new family's bonds and building new memories.

Dealing with Your Ex About Your Marriage—and Hers

It doesn't matter who finds a new partner first, you or your ex. Either way, remarriage is going to stir the pot that you've so carefully tended since your divorce.

When You Get Remarried

By the time you are ready to remarry, it's my sincere hope that you will have buried the hatchet with your former spouse and ended whatever domestic wars existed between you. With a little help from your friends, maybe the two of you are relating well enough that you would consider inviting her to your wedding. May it be so! But be prepared for a new round of stressful thoughts and tender feelings rising to the surface because your new marriage will send the final signal to all concerned that you and your ex are not getting back to-gether. This includes your kids, of course. But don't underestimate the impact on your ex, even though she may have moved on herself and already be in a new relationship.

Be mindful and considerate of your former spouse's feelings. After all, this is the person who once loved you and whom you once loved, and she is still connected to you as family through the children. Take the time to let her know about your upcoming marriage in person or with a special phone call. Don't let her hear it from your kids or another family member. Make sure she has the space to have her reactions, and make sure you tell her how much it would mean to you to have her blessing.

If your relationship with your ex is still strained, it's all the more important to be considerate about how you let her know you're getting married, but it's also important to maintain appropriate boundaries between you, so that issues between you and your ex don't start to be an issue in your new relationship.

True Stories: Setting Boundaries

"Judith, my ex, wanted to be invited to every family gathering," Shawn told a gathering of divorced fathers. "I did it for a while but she invariably made a scene, either getting into a crying jag or getting angry for some imagined or real slight on someone's part. My new wife hated it and was angry at me for even agreeing to let Judith attend these gatherings. My therapist told me I had to set limits with my ex and tell her that I found her behavior unacceptable. Well, she went through the ceiling with that, of course, and said that she was close to some of my other family members and I had no right to keep her away. But when she realized I was serious about holding to my demands, she apologized and we agreed that she'd attend only certain family gatherings—like our son's birthday and any reunion my Mom and Dad would be attending. My ex still keeps in touch with them. I think they like her better than me!"

When Your Ex Remarries

If your former wife remarries, it is bound to stir up some feelings in you, too. It might be that you still fantasize about getting back together. On the other hand, maybe you're ecstatic that someone is finally hooking up with her because maybe she'll stop calling you every time something needs to be fixed in the house. Whether you feel relieved or you are wondering why you are in grief, your ex getting married is bound to put you through some emotional changes.

Take a deep breath. Here is another opportunity for you to be a grownup and deal with life's tough transitions in a graceful manner. Think about the kids, and don't do anything that will embarrass them or make you feel ashamed or humiliated. While you don't have to be enthusiastic about your ex's marriage, you do need to be civil and not abandon your role as a strong and compassionate family leader. You might be unhappy and pissed off, but that doesn't give you the license to be a jerk. If her marriage triggers negative or just plain bewildering feelings, or you feel like you are just plain losing it, it's time to visit your therapist or a good friend with whom you can blow off some steam.

One of the things you may have feelings about is the idea of another man in the role of stepparent to your children—which of course is what will happen during the time that your kids are with their mom, just as your new partner spends time with your kids when they are with you. Here's where you may have to take an extra big breath and make the extra effort to put your kids' well-being before your own jealousy or concerns. Everyone involved will be challenged to make some adjustments. Don't forget that includes you!

True Stories: Called on the Carpet

A letter to Father.com presented the following problem: "My ex married a total a-hole and frankly I didn't want the guy within a mile of my kids. They invited me to their wedding but I didn't go. Over the past few months, Dale has left a dozen messages on my voice mail, wanting to get together with me. He says it's for the kids. The only thing I think would be good for the kids is if Dale got lost. Maybe I'm off the wall on this but I don't think so. What's other people's experiences with this kind of thing?"

Several other men sent in notes about their experiences, most of them recommending that the letter-writer agree to a meeting with the new spouse and find out what was going on. One cut right to the chase:

"Sounds like you're pre-judging Dale. Maybe he's an a-hole like you say, but I'm suggesting you could also be the bigger one here. Look, the guy is making an effort to bridge the canyon between you and him for the sake of your kid. I'd suggest getting off your high and mighty thing and at least giving this guy a chance. Just so you know, I come from a place of being in a similar place as you. I didn't speak to my ex or her old man for over a year after they got married. I got over myself when I saw my son and his stepdad getting along fine. In fact, since then his stepdad and I have become pretty good friends. He has two kids by a prior marriage, too, which makes me think we're all in this together and I'm not the only one who has ever gone through a divorce. Last summer I helped him build a playhouse at his ex's house, if you can believe that. It's been quite a journey. So, I say, lighten up and find out what's happening with this guy. There might be some good surprises in store for you and everybody involved."

Do We Really Have to Talk About This?

While you are making plans for your second marriage, the subject of prenuptial agreements might come up—and if you take my advice, you might be the first one to bring it up. If you've been through a nasty divorce, with battles over money and property, and have recovered financially, you might be particularly sensitive to this issue. For example, you might want to feel secure that a certain portion of your estate will go to your children when you die. If you have significant family assets or a family business, you might want to make certain that your interests and those of other family members are protected. If you are going to become a full-time stay-at-home parent, you will want to discuss how you and your fiancée view the meaning of equality. For example, what value will be placed on your labors at home? Are the family earnings going to be equally divided? Will decisions about spending be shared? And if your fiancée or you have contracts, debts, or have gone through bankruptcy recently, you may want to do something to keep your debts and financial responsibilities separate.

Why bring up money in a chapter dealing with love and the emotional issues surrounding a second marriage? Because money problems in a relationship can quickly turn into emotional problems. In fact, discussions around money will reveal a lot to you about how you and your fiancée view the financial partnership that is part and parcel of a marriage.

Initiating a discussion about a prenup isn't necessarily easy or comfortable. When we're in love, we don't want to talk about money. The best way to open such a discussion is not by introducing it as a prenuptial issue but as a discussion about values you both hold around what it means to have a true partnership. A conversation about your views of who owns what and what you and your fiancée view as equality in marriage can be one of the most important discussions you'll have.

Find out all you can about drawing up a prenuptial agreement before you sit down together for such a discussion. Then choose a time when you are both relaxed, and start out by saying something like, "I'd really like us to sit down and talk about our future together and the lifestyles we find comfortable as well as how we handle our finances. I want to talk about it now so it won't be hanging over our heads when we get married."

WHAT IS A PRENUP?

A prenuptial agreement, sometimes also called a premarital agreement, is a contract that partners draw up in anticipation of marriage, for the purpose of defining their financial rights and responsibilities during the marriage and also—yes, we need to say it—should the marriage not last. A prenup can limit the degree to which spouses share income or assets, or can define the amount of support that one spouse will pay the other after a divorce, or can provide that no support will be paid at all. Often, prenups list the assets that each person had before the marriage, and provide that those assets remain the separate property of the person who owns them, regardless of the state's law about sharing property during marriage.

Prenups are tailored to your situation, and you'll want to consult a lawyer for help in drafting one. But you can learn a lot about them from the book *Prenuptial Agreements: How to Write a Fair & Lasting Contract*, by Katherine E. Stoner and Shae Irving (Nolo).

Because the subject is uncomfortable, many people try to avoid direct discussions. But as often as not, avoidance tactics result in hard feelings or even the termination of a budding relationship. "I drew up my prenuptial and had my attorney send it to my fiancée," one man confessed. "And the outcome?" his friend asked. "Well, you'll notice I'm still single." A young attorney, after receiving a two-carat diamond ring and a proposal of marriage from her boyfriend, sat down two weeks later with him and asked him to discuss a prenup. After all, she said, she had royalty income from a book she'd written and regular monthly income from some property she'd sold and was carrying the financing on. Her friend became insulted and demanded the ring back. She was brokenhearted until a friend ran a credit check on the guy and found he'd gone through a bankruptcy only six months before—a small detail he'd avoided telling her.

Don't let a discussion about prenups fall to the bottom of your priority list just because you are uncomfortable talking about it. If there are details that are potentially problematic, it is much better to talk about them now rather than later. If you can't come to an agreement now, imagine what it could be like six months or a year from now when you discover that the money you pooled into your joint savings account is going to your new spouse's ex-husband who needed help buying a new car.

Nurturing Your Relationship

I close this chapter just as I opened it, with a reminder that the key to a healthy family is the mutual love, caring, and respect that the spouses bring to it. It's all too easy to forget in the midst of all the daily challenges and demands on us, that being alone together is essential. Take time to develop your bond independent of the children and the parenting roles and family tasks that make up your daily life. This is not a step that can be skipped! Getting away for a break may be difficult to arrange with all that's going on, but it is a key for building your own caring relationship, just the two of you. Making sure you do it will strengthen your ability to guide the new family.

Nurturing Your Extended Family

This entire book has been about ways to nurture the extended family that you will be creating after your divorce—the one that includes you, your kids, your ex, your new spouse and her family, your ex's new spouse and his family, your kids' grandparents, and of course, the family dog. The bottom line is to put your kids first, while making sure to take care of your own needs as well. Being a great dad during and after divorce can be challenging, but it brings home the reality that you are, in fact, always Dad. Good luck to you! ●

Divorce and Fathering Resources

Alliance for Non-Custodial Parents Rights

A nonprofit corporation dedicated to protecting and promoting the civil and inalienable human rights of noncustodial parents and their families. ANCPR also believes that it is in the "best interest of the child" to have equal access to both parents, and that shared custody arrangements that specify 50/50 joint physical custody should be the presumption in family law.

Website: www.ancpr.org
Contact: helpme@ancpr.org

American Coalition for Fathers and Children

Dedicated to the creation of a family law system, legislation, and public education that promote equal rights for all parties affected by divorce, the breakup of a family, or establishing paternity.

Website: www.acfc.org
Contact information:
1718 M. St. NW #187
Washington, DC 20036
Telephone: 800-978-3237
Fax: 703-442-5313

Boys to Men Mentoring Network

A program where boys between the ages of 12 and 16 can regularly interact with committed, conscientious adult men.

Website: www.boystomen.org
Contact information:
9587 Tropico Drive
La Mesa, CA 91941
Phone: 619-469-9599
Fax: 954-301-8115
email: boystomen@cox.net

Children's Rights Council

CRC works to assure a child the frequent, meaningful, and continuing contact with two parents and the extended family the child would normally have during a marriage.

Website: www.gocrc.com
Contact information:
6200 Editors Park Drive, Suite 103
Hyattsville, MD 20782
Phone: 301-559-3120
Fax: 301-559-3124

Divorced Fathers Network

Advocates of shared parenting, Divorced Fathers Network is dedicated to assisting fathers in parenting issues through a support group network, while helping men and women create cooperative parenting relationships with their former spouses.

Website: www.divorcedfathers.com
Contact information:
720 26th Ave #12, Santa Cruz, CA 95062
Phone: 831-335-5855
Email: steve@divorcedfathers.org

Dads And Daughters

A national education and advocacy nonprofit for fathers and daughters. DADs provides tools to strengthen father-daughter relationships and transform pervasive cultural messages that value daughters more for how they look than who they are.

Website: www.dadsanddaughters.org
Contact information:
2 West 1st Street, Suite 101
Duluth, MN 55802
Phone: 218-722-3942
Fax: 218-728-0314
Email: info@DadsAndDaughters.org

Father Resource Network

A national nonprofit organization whose mission is to provide a network of referral, resource, and support services that help solve the problems and challenges associated with fatherhood today.

Website: www.father.com
Contact information:
Box 126
Mill Valley, CA 94942
Phone: 415-381-1162
Email: paul@father.com

Fathers Matter

Father Matters is a nonprofit organization with the sole purpose of seeing that fathers become the best fathers they can be. Our main goal is to commit dads to encouragement, support, and accountability with other fathers, as well as themselves.

Website: www.fathermatters.com
Contact information:
P.O. Box 612473
San Jose, CA 95161-2473
Toll Free: 1-888-648-0718

Fathers Resource Center

Fathers Resource Center exists to provide the community with fathering information, education, support, and prevention programs focused on positive parenting.

Website: www.fathersresourcecenter.org
Contact information:
1020 Second St, Suite A
Encinitas, CA 92024
Phone: 760-634-3237

FatherNet

The electronic continuation of Family Re-Union III: The Role of Men in Children's Lives, a national conference on family policy moderated by Vice President Al Gore and co-sponsored by the Children, Youth and Family Consortium and the Tennessee Department of Human Services.

Website: www.cyfc.umn.edu
Contact information:
McNamara Alumni Center, Suite 270A
200 Oak Street S.E.
Minneapolis, MN 55455
Phone: 612-625-7849

Fatherville

An online community where fathers from all walks of life can learn from one another. It's only by relating our own personal tips, tricks and traps that we can learn about some of the pitfalls to be avoided.

Website: www.fatherville.com

Contact information:

Phone: 208-887-9086

MESA: Men's Educational Support Association

An organization whose main objective is to help families, fathers, and children caught in the turmoil of domestic crisis. We are a group of men and women in the community whose aims are to make available the emotional resources and legal referrals men require during a family breakdown.

Website: www.mesacanada.com

Contact information:

Box 4691, Stn 'C'

Calgary, Alberta

Canada T2T 5P1

Military Divorce Guide

A comprehensive guide to military divorce and family law issues, including the division of military retirement, VA disability, military family support, Servicemembers Civil Relief Act (formerly SSCRA), former spouse benefits, etc.

Website: www.military-divorce-guide.com

Contact information:

128 S. Tejon St., Ste 410

Colorado Springs, CO 80903

Phone: 719-630-8494

Fax: 719-630-8495

National Center for Fathering

NCF's mission is to inspire men to be better fathers. In response to a dramatic trend towards fatherlessness in America, the Center was founded in 1990 by Dr. Ken Canfield to conduct research on fathers and fathering, and to develop practical resources to prepare dads for nearly every fathering situation.

Website: www.fathers.com
Contact information:
P.O. Box 413888
Kansas City, MO 64141
Phone: 800-593-DADS
Fax: 913-384-4665
Email: dads@fathers.com

National Fatherhood Initiative

Father absence has been found to be a major cause of childhood poverty, and other at-risk factors. NFI provides data on the significance of fathers who remain connected to their families. This information is critical to policy makers on the federal and state levels to ensure that laws promote families and responsible father behavior.

Website: www.fatherhood.org
Contact information:
101 Lake Forest Boulevard
Suite 360
Gaithersburg, MD 20877
Phone: 301-948-0599
Fax: 301-948-4325

National Center on Fathering and Families

The mission of the National Center on Fathers and Families (NCOFF) is to improve the life chances of children and the efficacy of families and to support the conduct and dissemination of research that advances the understanding of father involvement.

Website: www.ncoff.gse.upenn.edu

Contact information:

University of Pennsylvania

3440 Market Street

Suite 450

Philadelphia, PA 19104-3325

Phone: 215-573-5500

Separated Parenting Access & Resource Center

Separated Parenting Access & Resource Center (SPARC) website is a nonprofit website with several specific mission goals, such as to assist fathers in obtaining legal custody of their children.

Website: www.deltabravo.net/custody

Contact information:

P.O. Box 82764

Kenmore, WA 98028-0764

The Single and Custodial Father's Network (SCFN)

Member supported nonprofit organization, dedicated to fathers who meet the challenge of custodial parenthood.

Website: www.scfn.org

Contact information:

900 Birch Drive

Cranberry Twp., PA 16066

Phone: 412-853-9903

Fax: 412-291-1771

SLOWLANE.com

Slowlane.com is the online resource, reference, and network for Stay At Home Dads (SAHD) and their families. The Slowlane.com site provides dads with a searchable collection of articles and media clips written by, for, and about primary caregiving fathers. It also hosts multiple websites for at-home dads, including independent SAHD groups and several local Dad-to-Dad chapters, all of whose missions are to help dads connect with each other in their local areas.

Website: www.slowlane.com
Contact information:
1216 East Lee Street
Pensacola FL, 32503
Phone: 850-434-7937
Fax: 850-434-2626

Stepfamily Association of America

A national, nonprofit membership organization dedicated to successful stepfamily living. Our site provides educational information and resources for anyone interested in stepfamilies and their issues.

Website: www.saafamilies.org
Contact information:
650 J Street, Suite 205
Lincoln, NE 68508
Phone: 800-735-0329

Remember:
Little publishers have big ears.
We really listen to you.

Take 2 Minutes
& Give Us
Your 2 cents

Your comments make a big difference in the development and
revision of Nolo books and software. Please take a few minutes
and register your Nolo product—and your comments—with us. Not only will
your input make a difference, you'll receive special offers available only to registered owners
of Nolo products on our newest books and software. Register now by:

PHONE
1-800-728-3555

FAX
1-800-645-0895

EMAIL
cs@nolo.com

or **MAIL** us
this registration card

- fold here -

NOLO
Registration Card

NAME _____ DATE _____

ADDRESS _____

_____

CITY _____ STATE _____ ZIP _____

PHONE _____ EMAIL _____

WHERE DID YOU HEAR ABOUT THIS PRODUCT? _____

WHERE DID YOU PURCHASE THIS PRODUCT? _____

DID YOU CONSULT A LAWYER? (PLEASE CIRCLE ONE)   YES   NO   NOT APPLICABLE

DID YOU FIND THIS BOOK HELPFUL?   (VERY)   5   4   3   2   1   (NOT AT ALL)

COMMENTS _____

_____

WAS IT EASY TO USE?   (VERY EASY)   5   4   3   2   1   (VERY DIFFICULT)

We occasionally make our mailing list available to carefully selected companies whose products may be of interest to you.

❑ If you do not wish to receive mailings from these companies, please check this box.

❑ You can quote me in future Nolo promotional materials.
   Daytime phone number _____.

DIFA 1.0

Nolo in the NEWS

"Nolo helps lay people perform legal tasks without the aid—or fees—of lawyers."

—USA TODAY

Nolo books are ..."written in plain language, free of legal mumbo jumbo, and spiced with witty personal observations."

—ASSOCIATED PRESS

"...Nolo publications...guide people simply through the how, when, where and why of law."

—WASHINGTON POST

"Increasingly, people who are not lawyers are performing tasks usually regarded as legal work... And consumers, using books like Nolo's, do routine legal work themselves."

—NEW YORK TIMES

"...All of [Nolo's] books are easy-to-understand, are updated regularly, provide pull-out forms...and are often quite moving in their sense of compassion for the struggles of the lay reader."

—SAN FRANCISCO CHRONICLE

fold here
- -

Place
stamp here

Nolo
950 Parker Street
Berkeley, CA 94710-9867

Attn: DIFA 1.0